A PRACTICAL GUIDE TO LEADING WITH HEART
AND STRENGTH

EMOTIONAL INTELLIGENCE

HOW TO BE A BRAVE, EMOTIONALLY STRONG LEADER

KARINA G. JAUREGUI

© Copyright 2025 Karina G. Jauregui - All rights reserved.

The content within this book may not be reproduced, duplicated, or transmitted without direct written permission from the author or the publisher.

This book is copyright-protected and intended for personal use only. You cannot amend, distribute, sell, quote, or paraphrase any part of its content without the author's or publisher's consent.

By reading this document, the reader agrees that, under no circumstances, the author is liable for any direct or indirect losses incurred from using the information contained herein, including errors, omissions, or inaccuracies.

Please note that the information in this document is for educational purposes only. Readers acknowledge that the author does not provide legal, financial, medical, or professional advice. The content of this book has been sourced from various authors.

Content

Introduction 5

Chapter 1: Foundations of Emotional Intelligence in Leadership 9

    Understanding Emotional Intelligence Frameworks 10

    The Science Behind Emotional Intelligence and Leadership 14

    Why Emotional Intelligence Matters 16

    Emotional Intelligence vs. Traditional Leadership Skills 18

    Identifying Your Leadership Style Through Emotional Intelligence . 20

Chapter 2: Self-Awareness and Personal Growth 25

    Reflection Section: Your Emotional Trigger Journal 28

    The Role of Self-Awareness in Effective Leadership 30

    Mindful Leadership: Clear Mind, Bold Moves 32

    Emotional Agility in Leadership 36

Chapter 3: Emotion Regulation and Stress Management 41

    The Impact of Emotional Control in Leadership 45

    Self-Regulation Techniques for High-Pressure Situations 48

    The Power of Emotional Resilience 51

    Balancing Emotions and Logic in Decision Making 54

    Cultivating a Positive Leadership Mindset 56

Chapter 4: Interpersonal Skills and Communication 61

    Building Genuine Connections with Your Team 64

    Bridging the Empathy Gap: Connecting with Your Team 67

    Communicating with Clarity and Empathy 69

    Feedback as a Tool for Growth and Connection 71

Enhancing Team Dynamics through Emotional Intelligence 74

Chapter 5: Conflict Resolution and Team Cohesion 81

Checklist for Preparing Difficult Conversations............................... 84

Root Causes of Workplace Conflicts 87

Conflict Resolution Strategies for Leaders 91

Building Trust and Credibility through Conflict Resolution 94

Emotional Intelligence in Negotiation and Mediation 96

Creating a Culture of Open Communication 99

Chapter 6: Building Trust Through Cultural Competence 103

Developing Cultural Competence as a Leader................................ 108

Overcoming Unconscious Bias with Emotional Intelligence 111

Chapter 7: How Emotionally Smart Leaders Rise in Crisis 115

How Empathy Beat Ego: A Leadership Story That Inspires 118

The Cost of Emotionally Unintelligent Leadership 122

Leadership Lessons from Emotional Intelligence Failures 124

Tailoring Emotional Intelligence to Your Industry......................... 126

Chapter 8: Sustaining Growth and Continuous Learning............. 129

Creating a Personal Growth Plan for Emotional Intelligence......... 130

Continuous Feedback Loops: Learning From Your Team 132

Staying Current: Emotional Intelligence Trends and Research 134

Leveraging Emotional Intelligence for Career Advancement 137

Conclusion 141

More Books by Karina G. Jauregui:... 145

References.. 147

INTRODUCTION

It was a rainy Tuesday—the kind of day that fogs up your windows and clouds your mind. Sarah sat at her desk, overwhelmed by messages, urgent emails, and an ever-growing to-do list. As a project manager at a leading tech firm, her role had always been intense, but today, it felt like she was caught in a storm she couldn't control. Deadlines loomed, team morale was declining, and for the first time, she questioned whether she was truly leading or just struggling to stay afloat.

Across the city, Alex was in a different office but a similar spiral—more spreadsheets than chat threads, yet the same weight pressing on his chest. As a finance executive, Alex was fluent in numbers, just as some people are fluent in emotions. But lately, those numbers weren't comforting—they were hollow. His team met targets but didn't talk. They executed plans but barely connected. And that quiet disconnection gnawed at him, even if he didn't say it out loud.

On paper, they were thriving. Promotions? Check. High-profile projects? Absolutely. Respect and recognition? Plenty. But beneath the surface, Sarah and Alex were wrestling with something success didn't protect them from: disconnection. From their teams. From their purpose. And, quietly, from themselves.

Then came a moment of coincidence—or perhaps fate.

Each discovered a course on emotional intelligence for emerging leaders—one that stood out not for its flash but for its depth. It offered a refreshing shift from surface-level tactics to something more meaningful: a way to lead with both heart and results. For Sarah and Alex, it was precisely the leadership reset they didn't know they needed.

They met on the very first day.

Sarah, all speed and spark, led with instinct and an extra shot of espresso. Alex, with all composure and calculation, led with logic and precision. On the surface, they were opposites. But when they talked, something clicked. They shared aspirations and exhaustion.

Through weeks of peer coaching, late-night reflections, and leadership "aha" moments that deeply affected them, they started a transformation—from the inside out. They didn't just study emotional intelligence. They embodied it. They learned to navigate stress without losing themselves, give feedback without fear, replace control with connection, and lead with clarity and compassion.

This book tells their story—not as a fairy tale but as a mirror of what leadership looks like when rooted in emotional depth. Through Sarah and Alex's journeys, you'll see how emotional intelligence shows up in real-life moments: awkward performance reviews, tense team meetings, early-morning burnout, and late-night wins. You'll witness what happens when leaders stop pretending to have it all together—and start leading from who they are.

Alongside their story, you will discover tools, reflection prompts, and strategies to apply these insights to your leadership journey.

The strongest leaders aren't the ones with all the answers, but the ones brave enough to look inward and ask the hard questions.

Modern leadership is about leading people, not merely managing projects. And it's about understanding your own emotions to help others succeed.

Leadership doesn't have to feel like a constant sprint. If you've been craving more clarity, connection, and courage in how you lead, this book is your moment. Think of it as your toolkit for leading with presence, your map for realignment, and a reminder that heart and results can go hand in hand.

Are you ready to lead with clarity, courage, and emotional depth?

Let's get started.

Chapter 1: Foundations of Emotional Intelligence in Leadership

"Leadership is not about being in charge. It's about taking care of those in your charge."
— Simon Sinek

Sarah sat at her desk, the low hum of servers blending with the sharp clicks of her team's keyboards. Everything appeared as it should from the outside—deadlines being met, sprints in motion, productivity humming along. But inside, she felt it again: that quiet tension in the air, the unspoken hesitations in meetings, the sense that her team was following orders, not following her. It wasn't resistance—it was disconnection.

Miles away, Alex flipped through another stack of quarterly reports. His office, though silent, echoed with pressure. Numbers told him they were hitting their goals, but the energy was off when he looked up at his team. They avoided eye contact, checked boxes, and kept things transactional. He missed the spark—the sense of unity, of people moving together toward something that mattered, somewhere along the way, that had slipped through his fingers.

Sarah and Alex had spent years honing their technical skills, leading projects, and managing deliverables. They knew how to hit targets. They didn't know how to rekindle a connection and lead in a way that inspired results, trust, respect, and engagement.

What they needed wasn't another leadership workshop filled with buzzwords and frameworks. They needed a new lens—a way to understand themselves and the people they led on a deeper level.

They needed emotional intelligence.

This chapter establishes the foundation for that journey. Through Sarah and Alex's experiences, we'll examine what emotional intelligence truly means in the context of leadership. Like Sarah and Alex, many leaders find that success on paper isn't sufficient. Authentic leadership begins from within.

Understanding Emotional Intelligence Frameworks

Let's begin with a truth that every leader eventually learns the hard way: emotional intelligence (EQ) is not a soft skill — it's a strategic necessity. It's not about simply *feeling* more; it's about *leading* better. Emotional intelligence provides a structured approach to recognizing, interpreting, and managing emotions—both your own and those around you. Think of it as the compass that keeps your leadership steady when the terrain becomes unpredictable.

Daniel Goleman's framework remains one of the most influential. He defines emotional intelligence through five core components: self-awareness, self-regulation, motivation, empathy, and social skills. For leaders, these are not optional qualities; they are the foundation of presence and influence. Self-awareness sharpens your understanding of your behaviors, self-regulation tempers reactions under pressure, motivation sustains perseverance, empathy builds trust, and social skills open the door to authentic collaboration. Goleman's model equips leaders to lead with authority and humanity, not by controlling others, but by first mastering themselves.

Meanwhile, the Four Branch Model developed by John Mayer and Peter Salovey offers a different angle. This model approaches emotional intelligence as a set of mental abilities: perceiving emotions accurately, using emotions to facilitate thought, understanding emotional nuances, and managing emotions effectively. Think of it as developing an internal emotional intelligence dashboard. In leadership, this means the ability to sense the emotional undercurrents in a room, align them with strategic goals, and make decisions that account for logic and emotion. Leaders applying Mayer and Salovey's model do not simply react; they *calibrate*.

Then we have the Bar-On Model of Emotional-Social Intelligence, which takes the conversation even further by emphasizing stress management, interpersonal relationships, and decision-making. This model acknowledges that leadership does not occur in isolation but under pressure and within complex human environments. Bar-On's perspective reminds leaders that managing emotions is only half the equation; maintaining personal resilience and fostering positive social interactions are equally vital. Leadership success is not measured solely by performance metrics but also by how well a leader maintains personal well-being and healthy team dynamics.

Each of these frameworks offers a unique blueprint. Goleman sharpens leadership presence. Mayer and Salovey enhance emotional processing and strategic agility. Bar-On strengthens resilience and social effectiveness. No single model holds all the answers — but together, they provide an invaluable foundation for navigating the emotional dimensions of leadership.

The next logical step is to begin with self-assessment. Before leaders can chart a course for growth, they must first understand where they currently stand.

Sarah discovered this firsthand. One afternoon, she completed the *MindTools Emotional Intelligence Quiz*, and the results were revealing. Her scores in emotional self-regulation were lower than she had anticipated. Suddenly, she understood why high-pressure situations often left her reactive rather than strategic. This insight wasn't discouraging; it was liberating. With clarity came the opportunity for intentional change.

Alex, on the other hand, gravitated toward the *Greater Good Science Center's EI Quiz*, intrigued by its focus on recognizing emotions in others. A naturally analytical thinker, Alex realized that while he excelled at problem-solving, he often overlooked the emotional context of meetings and conversations. The quiz results were a turning point, highlighting that leadership is not just about managing outcomes, but also about sensing and responding to the team's emotional needs.

Together, Sarah and Alex explored the *IHHP EQ Quiz*, which presented real-world leadership scenarios and illuminated where their instincts aligned with emotionally intelligent leadership — and where they fell short. These assessments were not judgments; they were mirrors. They allowed Sarah and Alex to see their emotional habits clearly and provided actionable insights to enhance how they led their teams, made decisions, and built relationships.

Self-assessments are not exams to pass or fail; they are invitations to grow.

For Sarah and Alex, these tools marked the beginning of a new phase of leadership — one anchored in authenticity, emotional clarity, and deeper human connection.

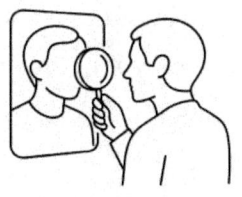

Now it's your turn. Take one of the free emotional intelligence assessments — MindTools, Greater Good, or IHHP — and see your current emotional blueprint. Just send me a quick email with the subject line "EQ Free Quiz" to **gjaureguikarina@gmail.com**, and I'll personally send you the links. What you discover might transform how you lead, how you connect, and how you inspire.

The Science Behind Emotional Intelligence and Leadership

Imagine you're at a meeting, the tension is palpable, and the air feels thick with unspoken words. You're about to speak when suddenly your heart races and your palms sweat. This is your amygdala at work, a part of the brain responsible for emotional reactions. It alerts you to potential threats, but sometimes it can overreact, like a fire alarm triggered by burnt toast. As a leader, understanding this instinctive response is crucial. Your prefrontal cortex, another brain region, steps in to help you think clearly and control impulses. It's the reason you don't yell at your boss or make rash decisions that could cost the company. Emotional intelligence is rooted in these brain functions, guiding you to react thoughtfully rather than impulsively.

Studies indicate a positive correlation between high EQ and enhanced team performance. Leaders who demonstrate emotional intelligence cultivate trust and open communication, leading to higher job satisfaction and reduced turnover rates. Imagine working for someone who genuinely listens and understands your concerns. This level of engagement boosts morale and translates into measurable business success. Teams led by emotionally intelligent individuals often outperform those guided by leaders who lack these skills.

Now, let's debunk some myths surrounding emotional intelligence. One common misconception is that it's purely innate—either you have it or you don't. This couldn't be further from the truth. Emotional intelligence is not fixed; it's a skill that can be developed over time through practice and self-awareness. Another myth suggests emotional intelligence lacks scientific backing. In reality, the field is backed by strong research that emphasizes its neurological foundations and practical uses in leadership contexts.

A study involving over 200 leaders across various industries found that those with high emotional intelligence achieved significantly better outcomes in decision-making, conflict resolution, and strategic thinking †[9]. These findings emphasize the significance of developing emotional intelligence as an essential aspect of effective leadership.

Just last quarter, Sarah faced a moment of crisis. A major client she had personally worked hard to retain sent an unexpected email threatening to terminate their contract due to a delayed feature rollout. Her first instinct was panic: a tightening in her chest, a dozen defensive responses forming in her mind. But instead of reacting, she paused. She knew her team would mirror whatever energy she brought into the room. Drawing on her growing emotional intelligence, she acknowledged her stress privately, then gathered her team with a calm, focused tone. Together, they assessed the situation, mapped out a solution, and initiated a direct and empathetic conversation with the client. The result? The relationship was preserved, the delivery was reorganized, and her team left feeling not stressed but empowered. Had Sarah let her emotions take over, the outcome might have been very different.

Emotional intelligence plays a crucial role in decision-making processes. Leaders who understand their emotional triggers can navigate complex situations with clarity and confidence. They evaluate options thoroughly, considering logical outcomes and emotional impacts on their teams. This balanced approach frequently results in improved decisions supporting organizational objectives and employee well-being.

Why Emotional Intelligence Matters

Many experienced leaders take pride in their management skills, often viewing emotional intelligence as merely a passing trend. "I'm already a good leader," they might say, confident in their ability to drive results and lead teams effectively. Yet, beneath the surface of this self-assurance lies a crucial oversight. Emotional intelligence is not just an optional skill; it's an impactful asset. It is the secret ingredient that sets great leaders apart from good ones. It represents the difference between merely managing a team and genuinely inspiring one.

Data consistently shows that leaders with high emotional intelligence foster more productive and engaged teams. According to a study by the Harvard Business Review, emotionally intelligent leaders can improve team performance by up to 20%. This isn't about jumping on the latest bandwagon but embracing a proven method for enhancing leadership effectiveness.

Emotional intelligence may seem less relevant in finance, where numbers dominate conversations and performance is measured in decimals and percentages. Alex used to believe that, too. As a finance executive, he prided himself on accuracy, efficiency, and delivering results. But over time, he began to notice something unsettling: his team was disengaged, turnover was rising, and collaboration had dwindled to a minimum. It wasn't that the numbers were off; the people behind them felt unseen.

After starting the emotional intelligence course, Alex consciously decided to shift his approach. He began scheduling one-on-ones to discuss deliverables and ask about stressors, motivation, and team dynamics. He listened to what his team was experiencing. He acknowledged their concerns without immediately jumping into problem-solving mode and responded with empathy instead of efficiency. Over time, trust began to build. Team members spoke up more often, morale improved, and the atmosphere shifted from tense to collaborative.

Productivity increased, miscommunications lessened, and decision-making became more inclusive and effective. What changed wasn't the financial model—it was the emotional foundation on which the team operated. Alex didn't abandon logic; he enhanced it with empathy.

Emotional intelligence allows leaders to respond thoughtfully rather than impulsively to challenges, ensuring that decisions align with business objectives and team well-being.

When was the last time you took a moment to ask yourself not what your team is doing, but how they're feeling?

Remember that emotional intelligence involves recognizing the potential within yourself and your team while creating an environment where everyone can succeed.

Emotional Intelligence vs. Traditional Leadership Skills

In today's whirlwind of leadership demands — where deadlines loom, inboxes overflow, and decisions must sometimes be made in the time it takes to sip a coffee — traditional leadership skills like strategic planning and technical expertise remain absolutely critical. These are the fundamental capabilities that enable organizations to operate and thrive. However, emotional intelligence brings a powerful, often underestimated, dimension to the leadership equation. It doesn't replace technical skills — it *amplifies* them, creating a more complete, human-centered approach to leading.

Think of it this way: technical skills teach you how to build a car with precision and efficiency. Emotional intelligence teaches you how to understand what it feels like to drive that car on a rainy night, tired after a long journey. One is about the mechanics; the other is about the experience. In leadership, both matter — but the emotional layer turns competent leadership into *transformational* leadership.

When emotional intelligence enters the picture, interpersonal skills don't just exist — they thrive. Leaders with high EQ navigate tricky team dynamics with finesse, mediate conflicts without leaving bruises, and earn trust without resorting to grand speeches. They become the kind of leaders others *want* to follow, not just *have* to follow.

Without emotional intelligence, even the most technically brilliant leader can find themselves isolated—respected perhaps, but not trusted, admired from a distance but rarely approached in moments that matter most. Emotional intelligence adds vibrancy, authenticity, and color to what would otherwise be a black-and-white portrait of leadership competence.

Integrating emotional intelligence into a solid skill set isn't just a nice-to-have anymore; it's non-negotiable. Especially in decision-making, emotional intelligence acts like a radar, picking up the subtle emotional signals that often swirl just beneath the surface. A leader attuned to these signals might sense unease in a team before rolling out a significant change. Rather than bulldozing ahead, they pause, address the concerns, and bring their people along, reducing resistance and increasing commitment. This kind of emotional foresight doesn't just prevent mistakes; it builds a culture where collaboration thrives because people feel seen and respected.

And then there's emotional empathy — the crown jewel of emotionally intelligent leadership. While traditional leadership often emphasizes efficiency and results, emotional empathy invites something deeper: real human connection. It's the ability to move beyond transactional conversations into relationships that foster loyalty, psychological safety, and authentic engagement. Leaders who demonstrate emotional empathy in high-pressure moments don't just stabilize the room — they reignite the team's energy and confidence.

Where others might see only challenges, empathetic leaders see opportunities for growth, resilience, and transformation. They are the ones teams rally around when the stakes are high, not because they command it, but because they have earned it.

In an era where technical skill is increasingly matched across competitors, emotional intelligence has become the great differentiator. It's not a soft luxury. It's a leadership superpower—subtle, powerful, and, once mastered, truly revolutionary.

Identifying Your Leadership Style Through Emotional Intelligence

Leadership styles can vary as widely as the colors in a paint palette. One leader might lean towards *transformational leadership*, which focuses on inspiring and motivating team members to achieve more than they thought possible. This style is often marked by a charismatic leader who encourages innovation and creativity, fostering an environment where new ideas are welcomed and pursued. On the other hand, some leaders might prefer a *transactional approach*, emphasizing structure, routine, and clear objectives. Here, rewards and penalties are the norm, providing a systematic way to achieve specific goals.

Emotional intelligence is crucial in determining which leadership style suits a leader best. It's like a compass that guides leaders through the complexities of managing diverse teams. For example, a transformational leader with high emotional intelligence can recognize when their team needs encouragement and when to step back to let creativity flourish. Conversely, a transactional leader who understands emotional cues can effectively use incentives to boost morale without stifling initiative. In both cases, emotional intelligence enhances the leader's ability to adapt their style to the needs of their team, creating a harmonious and productive work environment.

Adaptability is a hallmark of emotionally intelligent leaders. They can shift their leadership style to suit various situations, like a skilled driver adjusting their speed according to road conditions. For example, an emotionally intelligent leader might adopt a more authoritarian style in times of crisis, providing clear direction and making swift decisions to navigate turbulent waters. However, once the storm passes, they can seamlessly transition back to a more collaborative approach, encouraging team input and fostering a sense of collective responsibility.

This adaptability extends beyond crisis management. Consider a situation where a team works on a project with tight deadlines. An emotionally intelligent leader may initially take a transactional approach to ensure everyone is focused on meeting targets. Yet, as the project progresses, they might shift to a transformational style to keep motivation high and prevent burnout. This flexibility allows leaders to maintain momentum while addressing the evolving needs of their team.

Emotionally intelligent leaders understand that their actions and words can significantly influence team morale. Recognizing and responding to their team's emotional needs can create a supportive environment where individuals feel heard and respected. This sense of belonging encourages team members to collaborate more effectively, resulting in innovative solutions and improved performance.

Moreover, emotionally intelligent leadership promotes resilience within teams. When team members know they have a leader who genuinely cares about their well-being, they are more likely to persevere through challenges.

Alex was leading a high-stakes financial audit with tight deadlines. Naturally structured and results-driven, he leaned into a transactional style—clear tasks, strict timelines, and daily check-ins. But as the project wore on, he sensed growing tension and disengagement in the team.

Instead of tightening control, Alex applied his emotional intelligence. He paused to acknowledge the pressure, expressed appreciation, and invited feedback. That shift—small but intentional—reenergized the team. Morale improved, collaboration increased, and they completed the audit on time with fewer errors. By pairing structure with empathy, Alex proved that emotional intelligence can enhance even the most task-focused leadership style.

In such scenarios, emotional intelligence acts as a catalyst for positive change. It enables leaders to identify potential issues before they escalate, allowing for proactive solutions that enhance team dynamics. This proactive approach encourages a culture of continuous improvement, where feedback is welcomed and learning opportunities abound.

Identifying your leadership style through emotional intelligence is about understanding your strengths and areas for growth. It's about recognizing how different styles can be leveraged to achieve desired outcomes. Whether you naturally lean towards transformational or transactional leadership, integrating emotional intelligence into your approach will enhance your effectiveness.

As we've seen, emotional intelligence begins with a shift in perspective—a new lens through which leaders like Sarah and Alex are learning to connect with their teams more authentically. However, we must first understand ourselves before we can guide others with empathy and insight. In the next chapter, we will explore the foundation of emotional intelligence: self-awareness. You'll follow Sarah and Alex as they uncover the patterns behind their emotional reactions and discover how inner clarity becomes the foundation for lasting personal growth and decisive leadership.

TOP 3 TAKEAWAYS
(CHAPTER 1)

1   Emotional Intelligence Is a Strategic Leadership Asset, not a Soft Skill.

Emotional intelligence enhances—not replaces—technical expertise by helping leaders build trust, navigate team dynamics, and lead with authenticity. Frameworks like Goleman, Mayer-Salovey, and Bar-On offer structured ways to integrate EQ into leadership.

2   Self-Assessment Is the First Step Toward Change.

Tools like EQ quizzes offer leaders personalized insights into emotional habits and blind spots. These assessments act as mirrors, not report cards, guiding you toward meaningful self-improvement.

3   High EQ Leaders Inspire Teams Through Connection, Not Control.

Leadership success hinges on delivering results and emotional connection. Sarah and Alex learn that teams perform better when their emotional needs are acknowledged, leading to increased morale, stronger relationships, and more intelligent decision-making.

Chapter 2: Self-Awareness and Personal Growth

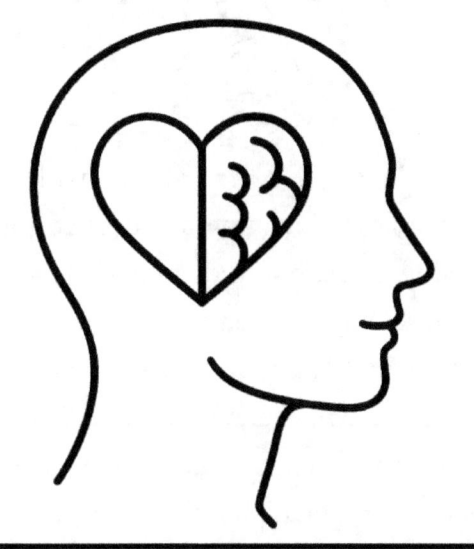

"Knowing yourself is the beginning of all wisdom." — Aristotle

Picture this: you're in the midst of a pivotal meeting, and suddenly, someone throws a curveball at you. Your pulse races, your cheeks flush, and it feels like the room's temperature has increased by ten degrees. Emotional triggers often drive moments when emotions flood in unexpectedly—those sneaky buttons that, once activated, can launch us into a whirlwind of reactions. Identifying these triggers is like discovering the user manual for our emotional selves.

This understanding provides invaluable insights into what triggers our responses, guiding us to the roots of our emotional disturbances.

Identifying emotional triggers starts with intentional self-observation. Imagine maintaining a dedicated journal—not for to-do lists or meeting notes, but to document the emotional moments that linger. What set you off today? Was it a colleague's dismissive tone? A last-minute alteration to a project you'd invested yourself in? These moments, while uncomfortable, are rich with insight. When recorded consistently, they begin to reveal patterns: situations, words, or behaviors that repeatedly provoke strong emotional responses.

Instead of viewing past disagreements as failures, consider them as data, each providing a clue about your emotional wiring.

- *What was truly behind your reaction? Was it the situation, or what it represented to you?*

- *What fear, value, or unmet need was stirred in that moment?*

These questions do more than help you decode your responses—they assist you in leading yourself better. And when you lead yourself with clarity, you fortify your ability to lead others with strength.

Comprehending the consequences of these triggers on your leadership style holds significant importance. Emotional hijacking occurs when these triggers disrupt your decision-making process, leading to impulsive or regrettable choices. Visualize standing at a metaphorical crossroads, where a split-second surge of emotion might steer you from a path of rationality. Recognizing this occurrence assists in reclaiming control, affording you the capacity to respond with deliberation and consideration rather than impulsiveness. Leaders who understand their emotional triggers can skillfully manage tense interactions with poise, reinforcing their authority and fostering trust.

Effective management of these triggers calls for strategic interventions. Among the available techniques, deep breathing stands out as remarkably effective. Simple yet impactful, deep breathing exercises can soothe your nervous system, offering a vital pause before formulating a response. Closing your eyes, taking a mindful inhale through the nose, briefly holding your breath, and exhaling gently helps shift the focus from the triggering event to a calm reflection. Meanwhile, cognitive reframing is instrumental in reshaping your approach to triggers. By modifying the way you perceive triggering events, it is possible to change your outlook from negative to a state that is neutral or even optimistic.

Reflection Section: *Your Emotional Trigger Journal*

Establish an emotional trigger journal to capture moments that provoke strong emotional reactions. In your journal, document:

- *The date and time of the event*
- *A brief description of the incident*
- *The emotion you felt*
- *What do you think caused that emotion*
- *How you reacted in the moment*
- *How you might handle it differently next time*

Sarah began journaling after a tough month of miscommunications with her engineering team. Her first few entries were raw—snap judgments she regretted, passive-aggressive email replies, moments of frustration she couldn't explain. But over time, a pattern became clear: moments of perceived disrespect—missed deadlines, vague answers—sparked a fear of losing control. That awareness was a turning point. She paused when triggered, often with a deep breath and a silent reminder: "This isn't personal." She rewired how she responded by processing these moments on paper.

This journey of self-awareness is not easy—it requires intention and honesty. However, its impact is substantial: enhanced decision-making, improved communication, and the calm confidence that arises from emotional clarity.

Managing emotional triggers is not about suppressing them but understanding them. By modeling calm under pressure, leaders like Sarah demonstrate what emotional maturity looks like. In doing so, they invite their teams to grow alongside them.

📄 *Exercise: Track Your Triggers*

Try this exercise over the next two weeks:

- Choose a small notebook or digital app to serve as your journal.
- Record at least one triggering moment daily.
- At the end of each week, reflect:
  - *What patterns are emerging?*
  - *What situations consistently activate strong emotions?*
  - *How are you growing in your response?*

This isn't just a journal—it's a mirror. The more clearly you see your emotional self, the more powerfully you lead.

The Role of Self-Awareness in Effective Leadership

Imagine trying to navigate a bustling city you have never set foot in, without the guidance of a map, GPS, or any local directory to assist you. Given enough time and persistence, you might make some headway, but there's a good chance you'd endure a fair amount of frustration from multiple wrong turns. Leadership, when pursued without self-awareness, mirrors this scenario quite closely. It resembles navigating the complex and ever-changing maze of corporate challenges blindfolded, missing the essential compass of introspection and self-reflection. Self-awareness is a guiding lighthouse in this labyrinth, illuminating the murky waters and helping you identify your strengths, recognize your limitations, and grasp how each directly contributes to the decision-making process.

This clear understanding enhances the quality of decisions and improves the decision-making process, ensuring that choices are based on knowledge and intentionality. Recognizing the consequences of one's choices provides a broader perspective on their ripple effects, showing how each decision affects the composition of one's team, aligns with organizational goals, and ultimately influences the organization's overall structure.

Empathy is often viewed as an outward expression, but it begins inward, with self-awareness. Leaders who develop a deep understanding of their own emotions and triggers naturally become more attuned to the emotional cues of others. This shift doesn't require dramatic gestures; it's built on the quiet power of presence, observation, and care. When leaders truly see their team, not just for what they do, but for who they are, it transforms the relational dynamic from transactional to human.

Alex experienced this firsthand. As someone who once prided himself on logic and data, he used to see emotions as distractions in high-stakes financial discussions. However, as he developed more self-awareness, particularly his tendency to dominate conversations when stressed, he began to recognize how often he missed valuable input. One day, during a strategy meeting, he noticed his usual pattern kicking in: pushing ahead, cutting in mid-sentence, and rushing to conclusions. But this time, he caught himself.

He paused, invited his junior analyst to finish her thought, and listened. What she shared reshaped the entire discussion. It wasn't just a good idea; it was a perspective he would have overlooked entirely. That moment stayed with Alex. He realized empathy wasn't about having the right words but making space for others to be seen and heard.

Empathy, grounded in self-awareness, became Alex's superpower. By recognizing his emotional tendencies and adjusting his behavior, he unlocked hidden strengths within his team. Their sense of trust and inclusion grew, and the overall culture shifted from compliance to shared ownership.

Self-aware leaders like Alex don't just manage—they connect. That connection turns a group of individuals into a high-performing, unified team.

Mindful Leadership: Clear Mind, Bold Moves

Imagine the chaos of a typical workday, with its lively mix of noise and endless demands: the incessant ringing of the phone, the constant influx of emails clamoring for attention, each message carrying its sense of urgency, and the to-do list that seems to grow longer with each passing moment. In this whirlwind, finding your center might seem daunting, if not impossible. This, however, is where mindfulness steps in—not as a magical solution that wipes away the chaos—but as a practical and grounded tool that aids you in navigating the storm with enhanced clarity and poised elegance. Mindfulness, in its essence, *is the practice of being fully present in the moment, engaging wholeheartedly with your surroundings without casting any shadows of judgment.* For leaders, this means approaching each interaction, every challenge, or decision with a laser focus and clear-mindedness. It's about cultivating a calm and centered presence, even when the world seems spinning out of control.

In leadership, mindfulness translates into a heightened awareness, not just of one's own emotions that fluctuate with the tides of daily stressors, but also of the dynamics at play within the ecosystem of your team. A mindful leader embodies active listening during meetings, perceives subtle signs of distress in a team member's demeanor, and responds with compassionate empathy and composed understanding. By embracing mindfulness, you enhance your leadership presence and become a beacon of inspiration, instilling confidence and fostering trust. Your team looks to you, seeking direction and reassurance, sensing that at the core of challenges lies a calm center of certainty. Like an unyielding anchor in a storm, mindfulness keeps you steady amid the turbulent waves of change and transformation.

Integrating Mindfulness doesn't require incense, silence, or hours of meditation. For leaders navigating full schedules and constant demands, incorporating mindfulness into daily life is more about intentional moments of presence than dramatic lifestyle changes.

Think of mindfulness as showing up fully in the moment—whether that moment is a tense team meeting or your first sip of tea in the morning. When embedded into your day, these micro-practices become anchors that steady you amid chaos.

Let's explore two powerful, accessible techniques and how to incorporate them into your routine:

---

1. Mindful Breathing: Your Built-in Reset Button

It's a simple breathing practice that brings awareness to your inhale and exhale, helping quiet the mental noise and reduce reactivity.

How to do it:

- Sit upright, close your eyes if you're comfortable.
- Inhale slowly through your nose for a count of 4.
- Pause for a moment at the top of the breath.
- Exhale gently through your mouth for a count of 4.
- Repeat this cycle for 2–3 minutes, allowing distractions to float by without judgment.

When to use it:

- Before walking into a meeting.
- After a difficult email.
- When transitioning between tasks.

Example: Sarah uses this technique in the two minutes between virtual meetings. Rather than jumping from one call to the next, she resets her energy and focus with five deep breaths. It's become her mental reboot—short, quiet, and effective.

---

2. Body Scan Meditation: *Grounding Through Awareness*

It is a guided attention exercise that helps you reconnect with your body, reduce physical tension, and bring your mind back to the present.

How to do it:

- Lie or sit comfortably in a quiet space.
- Begin by focusing on your toes. Notice any sensation—warmth, tightness, tingling.
- Slowly shift your attention up the body: legs, hips, abdomen, chest, shoulders, arms, neck, and the top of your head.
- As you scan, breathe into areas of tension and invite relaxation.

When to use it:

- Before bed to wind down.
- Midday to release accumulated tension.
- After a high-stress event like conflict resolution or crisis management.

Example: Alex does a 10-minute body scan during lunch breaks. It helps him reset physically and emotionally before tackling the second half of the day. After three weeks, he noticed better focus and improved emotional tone in his team interactions.

Mindfulness becomes most powerful when practiced **consistently**, not perfectly.

Here's a way to incorporate it into your routine:

- **Anchor it to an existing habit:** Try five mindful breaths while waiting for your coffee to brew.
- **Use reminders:** Place a small sticky note on your screen with the word "breathe."
- **Create rituals:** Begin your workday with a 2-minute breathing pause. End it with a short reflection: *What went well today? What did I learn?*

Mindfulness isn't just a personal wellness tool—it's a strategic leadership advantage. When you're present, you make better decisions, listen more deeply, and respond rather than react.

As you strengthen this practice, you'll notice subtle shifts: reduced reactivity, increased clarity, and a heightened sense of groundedness even on chaotic days. These aren't merely moments of stillness—they're moments of power.

Emotional Agility in Leadership

One of the most significant challenges leaders face is staying clear-headed and effective while navigating emotional complexity. This is where emotional agility becomes indispensable. It's not about suppressing emotions or letting them run wild. It's about staying connected to your feelings without being controlled by them. It's the ability to move through emotional experiences with curiosity, not rigidity; and clarity, not reactivity.

Think of emotional agility as the mental flexibility behind wise leadership. When you're emotionally agile, you don't ignore your stress, frustration, or fear—you acknowledge it, step back, and choose your response based on your values, not your reflexes. This allows a leader to say, "Yes, this is hard—and here's how we move forward," instead of reacting defensively or shutting down.

Sarah discovered this during a period of organizational restructuring. As roles shifted and uncertainty grew, her team looked to her for direction. Inside, she felt uneasy about her job security and the team's morale. But instead of pretending everything was fine or making reactive decisions, she paused. She admitted to herself that she was feeling anxious. She named it. She sat with it. And only then did she step into action: checking in with her team individually, gathering their feedback, and helping shape the transition with transparency and empathy. That internal flexibility—acknowledging her discomfort without letting it dictate her behavior—was emotional agility.

Leaders who cultivate emotional agility are better equipped to:

- **Adapt quickly to change** without losing sight of what matters
- **Navigate conflict** without defensiveness or blame
- **Make decisions** that consider both logic and emotional impact
- **Stay genuine** when facing challenges.

This agility is especially crucial in moments of tension. Where rigid leaders resist feedback or push harder to control outcomes, emotionally agile leaders pause and re-center. They ask:

- *What am I feeling?*
- *Why do I feel this way?*
- *What's the best way to respond in alignment with my values and goals?*

Over time, this self-inquiry becomes second nature. It prevents impulsive reactions and encourages thoughtful, grounded leadership—even in chaos.

Importantly, emotional agility is not about being "emotionally perfect." It's about being emotionally honest and mentally adaptable. It means allowing space for discomfort without becoming consumed by it. It means holding conflicting thoughts without forcing immediate resolution. The mindset allows leaders to stay creative in complexity and human in high performance.

And it's contagious. Teams led by emotionally agile leaders tend to be more open, resilient, and collaborative. Why? Because they're watching a leader who is not afraid to feel, pause, or adjust. That kind of modeling builds trust and permits others to lead themselves well.

So, as you continue your leadership journey, consider this:

- When confronted with resistance, how do you react?
- Do you allow yourself to feel uncomfortable before proceeding?
- Can you reframe your perspective on a situation, without compromising your values?

Emotional agility isn't a trait you either have or don't. It's a skill that starts with self-awareness and is sharpened by practice. And when mastered, it becomes one of the most empowering tools a leader can carry.

In the next chapter, we'll explore interpersonal communication—how to stay composed and connect deeply with others to build trust and collaboration.

Top 3 Takeaways
(Chapter 2)

1 Emotional Triggers Are Your Leadership Clues, Not Your Enemies

Your strongest emotions are signposts pointing to unmet needs, fears, or values. Tracking them with curiosity, not judgment, helps you lead yourself first and others better.

2 Mindfulness Turns Everyday Moments into Leadership Mastery

Simple, consistent mindfulness practices — like deep breathing or body scans — sharpen your focus, build resilience, and help you stay fully present, even in chaos.

3 Emotional Agility is the Superpower Behind Calm, Flexible Leadership

The best leaders aren't emotionless — they are emotionally agile. They feel discomfort, stay grounded, and choose their responses based on values rather than reflexes, modeling maturity that builds trust and resilience in their teams.

CHAPTER 3: EMOTION REGULATION AND STRESS MANAGEMENT

"Between stimulus and response there is a space. In that space is our power to choose our response."
— Viktor E. Frankl

Sarah stood at the head of the conference room table, surrounded by a dozen eyes on her every word. The client had flown in unexpectedly, and the presentation had changed overnight. Her team was exhausted, and tension hummed just beneath the surface. She could feel her pulse quicken; her thoughts momentarily scattered. In that moment, she wasn't just leading a project—she was holding the emotional center of the room. How she managed her stress would ripple through every person watching.

As a leader, these moments are part of your journey. High-stakes meetings, looming deadlines, and interpersonal conflicts—each scenario challenges your intellect and emotional regulation. Staying composed and thinking clearly under pressure isn't just helpful; it's essential. Effective emotion regulation allows leaders to resolve tension, lead with clarity, and create psychologically safe environments even in chaos.

One of the most overlooked yet powerful strategies is intentional time management. By prioritizing tasks and aligning them with your peak productivity hours, you protect space for strategic thinking. Delegation is equally vital—not as a sign of weakness, but as a strength that empowers others and reinforces trust. Sarah learned this during a product launch when she realized her need to control every detail stifled her energy and her team's autonomy. Releasing that grip didn't just reduce her stress; it invited collaboration.

Setting realistic expectations—for yourself and your team—also plays a critical role in stress regulation. The pursuit of perfection can silently breed burnout. However, when leaders acknowledge that mistakes are part of growth, they foster an environment where creativity thrives.

Of course, the mind-body connection is equally important. Regular movement, even a short daily walk, helps clear mental clutter and restore perspective. Nutrition, too, fuels clarity—supporting not just your body, but your capacity to show up fully in your leadership role.

Creating a personalized stress management plan ensures these strategies become habits, not just ideals. When leaders like Sarah commit to sustainable practices, they don't just strengthen themselves—they model resilience for their teams, building cultures where well-being and high performance coexist.

Stress Management Plan Template

Use this 4-step template to create a realistic and personalized plan to manage stress effectively and lead with clarity—even under pressure.

Step 1: **Identify Your Stressors**

- Reflect on the typical sources of stress in your role.
- Look at recent high-pressure moments. What triggered your stress response? Were there patterns?

Example: Alex realized he felt most stressed during end-of-quarter reviews, especially when data presentations were unpolished or rushed. The trigger wasn't just the numbers—it was a fear of being perceived as unprepared in front of senior leadership.

Step 2: **Set Goals**

- Define specific, realistic goals for reducing stress.

- Include both short-term goals (e.g., better handling a recurring stressor) and long-term goals (e.g., creating a balanced routine that supports resilience).

Example: Alex set a short-term goal of preparing review materials 48 hours in advance, and a long-term goal of improving his emotional response in high-stakes presentations through weekly reflection and breathing exercises.

Step 3: **Develop Strategies**

- Choose tactics that align with your leadership style and personal preferences.
- Include a mix of proactive techniques, such as strategic time blocking, delegation, physical activity, mindfulness, or daily walks.
- Schedule intentional breaks and non-negotiable moments of pause throughout your week.

Example: Alex began time-blocking two "quiet work" hours each morning for strategic prep. He also committed to three 15-minute weekly midday walks to reset and recharge.

Step 4: **Monitor Progress**

- Track how you're feeling over time through journaling, notes, or even a simple 1–10 rating.
- Review what's working—and where tweaks are needed. Let the plan evolve with you.

Example: After four weeks, Alex noted that he was feeling less overwhelmed and more present in team meetings. However, he noticed his walks were slipping on busy days, so he moved them to his calendar as recurring, protected appointments.

By walking through this plan and adjusting as needed, you'll begin transforming stress into something you manage, rather than something that manages you. Even more importantly, you'll model balance and emotional intelligence for your team, showing them what sustainable leadership looks like in action.

The Impact of Emotional Control in Leadership

Proper emotional regulation isn't about suppressing what you feel—it's about channeling those emotions to serve your leadership, your team, and the moment. In emotionally charged environments, your ability to remain composed becomes more than a personal strength; it becomes a strategic leadership asset. While self-awareness tells you *what* you're feeling, emotional control helps you decide *what to do with it*.

For leaders like Alex, this distinction became clear during a particularly tense moment. During a quarterly finance review, a senior executive publicly questioned the integrity of a key financial forecast in front of the entire department. Alex felt his heart rate spike. He could sense his team's eyes flicking toward him, waiting to see what would happen next.

He might have cut in defensively or allowed frustration to color his tone in the past. But that day, something was different. He paused, took a single deep breath, and centered himself. Instead of reacting, he responded: "That's a fair concern—let's take a closer look after this meeting and walk through the data together." With that, he gently moved the meeting forward. No drama. No damage. Just grounded, confident leadership.

That moment wasn't just about protecting a number on a spreadsheet. It was about setting the emotional temperature in the room—and showing the team what leadership looks like when things get uncomfortable.

This is the often-unseen impact of emotional control: you become the emotional anchor others hold onto. When everything feels uncertain, people naturally look to the leader not for perfection, but for *presence*. They want to see someone who can stay centered, think clearly, and guide others through turbulence with confidence and care.

Leaders who consistently regulate their emotions do more than project stability—they shape culture. Their steady energy becomes a cue for the team: *We're okay. We can handle this. Let's move forward together.* This builds trust, encourages open communication, and reinforces a culture where people feel psychologically safe, even when stakes are high.

But let's be clear—emotional control doesn't mean you don't feel deeply. It means you've built the muscle to step back, observe the feeling, and then choose a thoughtful response. It's not about hiding emotion; it's about harnessing it.

Techniques like cognitive reframing allow leaders to shift from reactive stories (e.g., *"This is a disaster"*) to empowering perspectives (e.g., *"This is a challenge we're equipped to learn from."*)

Emotionally regulated leaders create ripple effects far beyond the moment. Their ability to stay composed under pressure inspires calm, focus, and resilience in others. Over time, this consistency earns respect, not just for their competence but also for their character.

So, ask yourself:

- What happens when tension enters the room—do you amplify or absorb it?
- What emotional tone are you setting for your team, even before you speak?
- How do your reactions teach others how to show up in crisis?

Because here's the truth: people don't remember every decision you make—but they'll always remember how you made them *feel* when the pressure was on.

Emotional control is your steady hand at the helm. It anchors your leadership in presence and trust. When practiced regularly, it becomes a quiet superpower—one that turns everyday moments into opportunities to lead with depth, stability, and heart.

Self-Regulation Techniques for High-Pressure Situations

Imagine you're the captain of a ship caught in a storm. The waves crash, the wind howls, and all eyes are on you. Your team watches closely—not for orders but for your composure. How you react sets the tone. This is where self-regulation becomes your anchor.

Self-regulation is managing your emotional responses, especially in high-stress or high-stakes situations. It's not about suppressing your emotions but choosing how and when to express them. Think of self-regulation as your internal thermostat—it doesn't stop the heat from rising, but it keeps your response steady and functional.

Let's look at three proven techniques for building self-regulation, how they work, and how to apply them in real-world leadership situations.

1. Progressive Muscle Relaxation (PMR)

It is a stress-reduction technique where you intentionally tense and then release each muscle group in your body, one at a time.

How to apply:

- In a private setting or even at your desk, sit or lie down comfortably.
- Begin at your feet: curl your toes tightly for 5 seconds, then release.
- Move up to your calves, thighs, abdomen, and shoulders—tensing and releasing each area.

- Breathe deeply throughout the process.

When to use it:

Before high-stakes presentations, difficult conversations, or conflict mediation. Even 5 minutes of PMR before a stressful event can lower anxiety and increase mental clarity.

Example:

Sarah uses PMR five minutes before her weekly stakeholder calls. She locks her door, turns off notifications, and runs through the muscle sequence. The result? She enters the virtual room calm, confident, and focused.

---

2. Visualization (Guided Imagery)

Mentally transporting yourself to a calming setting to regulate stress and refocus your thoughts.

How to apply:

- Close your eyes and picture a peaceful place—a beach, a forest, a quiet library.
- Engage your senses. What do you hear? Smell? Feel under your feet?
- Stay in this mental space for a few minutes, breathing slowly and deeply.

When to use it:

Right after a conflict or when you're emotionally triggered and need to reset before making a decision or responding.

Example:

Alex visualizes standing on a mountain trail whenever a negotiation turns tense. This short mental reset helps him avoid frustration and respond with clarity and empathy.

---

3. Name It to Tame It (Emotional Labeling)

It is a neuroscience-backed practice of consciously identifying what you're feeling to reduce its intensity.

How to apply:

- Pause and ask yourself: *"What am I feeling right now?"*
- Be specific. Not just "stressed"—try "I feel overwhelmed because of time pressure."
- Acknowledge it internally or say it out loud if appropriate.

When to use it:

In the middle of an intense team meeting or during conflict, when your emotions start to take over.

Example:

In a heated budget review, Sarah notices her pulse rising. She silently tells herself, *"I'm feeling defensive because my proposal is being challenged."* That awareness calms her enough to stay engaged without lashing out.

Mastering self-regulation isn't just about personal composure—it creates a **ripple effect**. When your team sees you stay grounded under fire, they feel safer and more confident. You become the calm eye of the storm.

Don't wait for a crisis to practice. These skills, like muscles, strengthen with repetition. Build time into your daily routine—even 5 minutes can build resilience.

The Power of Emotional Resilience

Emotional resilience is the ability to recover swiftly from adversity. It's not about avoiding challenges but facing them head-on, learning, and emerging stronger. For leaders, emotional resilience is a buffer against the inevitable setbacks in any professional journey. Imagine you're in charge during a critical project, and everything that could go wrong does. Instead of succumbing to frustration, emotional resilience empowers you to regroup, reassess, and proceed with renewed focus. This bounce-back ability differentiates leaders who thrive from those who merely survive.

Alex experienced this during the launch of a high-profile initiative. After months of planning, the rollout was riddled with unexpected glitches—data errors, vendor delays, and public scrutiny from executives. Initially, the weight of disappointment hit him hard. But

instead of shutting down, he took an evening to reflect, journal, and speak with a trusted mentor. The next morning, he returned to the office with renewed clarity. He gathered his team, owned the situation without blame, and asked, "What's within our control today?" That shift in focus—from failure to forward momentum—sparked a wave of collaboration. Within two weeks, they had restructured the plan, recovered key deliverables, and regained leadership's trust.

Resilient leaders exhibit certain traits that set them apart. One of these defining characteristics is persistence. When obstacles arise, they don't retreat—they tackle challenges with determination. They view hurdles as opportunities for growth rather than insurmountable barriers. Optimism is another key trait. Even in the face of adversity, resilient leaders maintain a positive outlook. They believe in the possibility of success and inspire the same belief in their teams. This optimism fuels their persistence, creating a virtuous cycle of resilience and achievement.

Alex's story didn't end with a perfect outcome, but it ended with a stronger team and a deeper trust in his leadership. That's the essence of resilience: not bouncing back to where you were but bouncing forward to who you're becoming.

Leaders can adopt several strategies to build this kind of resilience. Developing a growth mindset is vital—seeing challenges as springboards rather than threats. By embracing learning opportunities, leaders cultivate long-term emotional strength. Building a supportive network is also crucial. Surrounding yourself with people who offer encouragement and perspective gives you a cushion of support when the pressure rises.

Setbacks are inevitable in leadership. They test resolve and character. However, resilient leaders view failures as temporary stepping stones toward deeper growth. Consider Walt Disney, who faced multiple rejections before building his iconic empire. Despite the odds, his persistence is a timeless example of the power of resilience.

Developing emotional resilience doesn't mean avoiding discomfort. It means learning how to move through it constructively. When faced with a setback, pause. Reflect on what happened, what you felt, and what you can take from the experience. That moment of introspection turns adversity into an investment in future strength.

Integrate resilience into your daily practices to make it part of your leadership identity. Start each day by revisiting a past challenge you've overcome—it's a reminder of your capacity to adapt and endure. Carve out time for self-care activities that refill your emotional tank: a morning walk, journaling, meaningful conversation, or time with loved ones. These small rituals build your reserves and prepare you to lead through adversity with grounded confidence.

Resilience isn't about being impervious to hardship—it's about being responsive to it. The most admired leaders aren't the ones who never fall; they're the ones who get back up, again and again, and bring others with them. Welcome your setbacks as part of your story—and show your team what it looks like to grow through the storm.

Balancing Emotions and Logic in Decision Making

Making decisions is one of the most critical leadership responsibilities, and often one of the most complex. The best choices aren't just made with cold logic or pure emotion, but with a thoughtful balance. Whether navigating a major transition or responding to a crisis, combining clear analysis with emotional insight can make the difference between a decision that merely works on paper and inspires trust, alignment, and lasting results. Emotional intelligence plays a key role here, helping you recognize how a decision will affect outcomes and people.

Sarah faced this during a vendor transition that her team had resisted for months. On paper, the new vendor was the better choice—lower cost, faster service. But something wasn't sitting right. Instead of pushing the change through, Sarah paused. She met with her leads not to defend the numbers, but to listen. A strong emotional tie surfaced to the current vendor, who had supported them through past crises and built personal relationships with the team. The resistance wasn't just about logistics—it was about loyalty. Informed by that insight, Sarah didn't reverse the decision but changed how she rolled it out. She invited team input, communicated openly, and introduced the change gradually. The result wasn't just operational—it was cultural. Her team felt seen, and their trust in her deepened.

One simple tool to help find this balance is a list of pros and cons with emotional impact. Beyond tracking benefits and risks, reflect on how each option might affect morale, energy, or alignment with your values. Ask yourself: *How would this choice feel for the people involved? What's the potential emotional cost—or gain?* Another helpful strategy is a decision matrix assigning weight to rational and emotional factors. This helps clarify situations where numbers alone don't tell the whole story.

Emotionally intelligent leaders also know how to listen to their gut—but not blindly. They treat intuition as a signal, not a shortcut. It's the starting point for asking better questions, not the final answer. When acknowledged and not ignored, emotions become a guide, not a distraction. For example, during times of change, leaders can often sense anxiety building before it's voiced. Checking in early helps prevent resistance later.

People are more likely to support decisions when they feel their perspective was considered. As Sarah's experience showed, honoring the emotional side of decisions doesn't slow things down—it creates smoother, more sustainable progress.

To build this skill, try keeping a decision journal. After each major decision, take a few minutes to reflect:

- What facts influenced your choice?
- What emotional dynamics did you notice?
- What would you do differently next time?

Over time, this reflection strengthens your ability to lead with clarity and empathy.

Balancing emotion and logic doesn't require compromising either. It involves leading with your entire self—your analysis, instincts, and understanding of how people are impacted. That's what transforms everyday decisions into significant moments of leadership.

Cultivating a Positive Leadership Mindset

Leadership isn't just about strategy and spreadsheets—it's also about vibes. Walk into a room with tension in your shoulders, and guess what? Your team will feel it before you even speak. That's why your mindset matters more than most people realize. A positive leadership mindset isn't about sugarcoating problems or putting on a fake smile. It's about choosing how you show up when things get real. It's about finding the courage to say, "This is hard… but we've got this." Positivity, when it's genuine, is powerful. It helps you steady the room,  motivate people, and turn frustrating moments into forward movement. In short? How you think becomes how you lead—and people are watching.

During the course, Sarah and Alex quickly discovered they were opposites in personality but twins in ambition. She was fast-talking and tech-focused, often leading with instinct and fire. He was methodical, finance-driven, and deliberate, calculating risks like a chess player. But by week three of the course, something had shifted. They'd partnered up for a peer feedback exercise, and what started as a required assignment turned into weekly check-ins and shared late-night texts about messy meetings, misunderstood intentions, and the exhaustion of trying to "hold it all together" as leaders.

Their connection deepened after the course ended. They started calling each other their unofficial "mindset coach." Every Monday morning, they'd hop on a 20-minute video call—not to review goals or strategies, but to ask one question: "Where's your head at?"

One Monday, Alex joined the call earlier than usual. He appeared calm yet somewhat distant.

"Got a big presentation today?" Sarah inquired.

"Yeah," he responded. "But honestly, I feel behind already. I've been grappling with everything I didn't complete last week."

Sarah took a moment. "Alright, let's change our mindset. What went well?"

Alex paused before saying, "I identified an error in the cash flow model before it reached the board… and I assisted one of my analysts in preparing for her first meeting with investors."

Sarah raised an eyebrow. "That sounds like leadership to me."

That reframe resonated with Alex. He recognized that his usual focus was on productivity, but his team needed him to be present. That day, he approached the presentation feeling grounded, concentrating on what he had contributed rather than what he hadn't.

This simple shift in mindset not only improved his mood but also enhanced his leadership. It reminded him that progress is more valuable than perfection.

Simple practices like daily gratitude reflections—writing down three things you're proud of or grateful for—can shift your energy quickly. Pair them with short affirmations like "I lead with clarity and care" or "I grow through challenge," and give your brain a new pattern to follow when stress appears.

And here's the thing: positivity is contagious. When you show up with calm conviction and possibility—even if you're tired—your team feels it. This creates a culture where people aren't just coping; they're contributing—not because everything's perfect, but because they believe in the mission *and* the mindset driving it.

To keep your leadership energy aligned, try these deeper mindset check-in questions each week:

- *What kind of energy have I been bringing into the room—and how is it affecting others?*
- *Have I been choosing courage over comfort in thinking, speaking, and leading?*
- *What belief do I need to let go of—or lean into—to lead from a place of strength this week?*

Write your answers down. Let them guide your tone, your strategy, and your presence.

A strong mindset doesn't mean you never feel discouraged; you know how to reset. It becomes a leadership identity, not just a performance. And the more you model that, the more your team learns to do the same.

As we close this chapter on emotional regulation and stress management, remember: your mindset fuels it all. It turns pressure into progress. It sets the emotional tone for how people show up around you. And it keeps your leadership grounded in clarity, even when chaos knocks at the door.

Next, we'll explore the power of interpersonal communication—how to connect more deeply with your team, strengthen trust, and lead with emotional intelligence in every conversation. When leaders learn to speak with intention, they unlock the full potential of the people around them.

TOP 3 TAKEAWAYS
(CHAPTER 3)

1   Emotional control isn't about being calm but choosing your impact.

In high-pressure moments, how you respond becomes the emotional cue for everyone watching. Leaders who regulate their reactions don't suppress emotions — they use them with intention to set the tone, protect trust, and lead with grounded presence.

2   Stress doesn't disappear, but you can outsmart it.

Whether it's deep breathing, time blocking, or walking briskly, managing stress is about building habits that protect your clarity and energy. Wise leaders know that sustainable performance starts with personal balance, not burnout.

3   Emotional resilience transforms setbacks into leadership strength.

Challenges and crises don't define your leadership—your response does. Resilient leaders absorb tension, adapt with clarity, and turn adversity into momentum that strengthens both themselves and their teams.

Chapter 4: Interpersonal Skills and Communication

"The most important thing in communication is hearing what isn't said." — Peter Drucker

Let's be honest—most people don't listen to understand; they listen to respond. However, true leadership begins when you stop crafting your reply and start genuinely paying attention.

Active listening isn't just a leadership technique—it's an emotional commitment. It means showing up fully, listening with your eyes and ears, and making people feel seen, not scanned. When you get it right, it transforms conversations from mechanical check-ins into moments of trust.

For Sarah, this realization came during a sprint review when her UX lead, Jenna, spoke up about constant last-minute scope changes. In the past, Sarah might've nodded and rushed to problem-solving. But this time, she leaned in and said, "It sounds like you're feeling unprepared and unheard. Is that right?" Jenna blinked, then exhaled. "Yes. Exactly." That moment shifted the dynamic. It wasn't about feature deadlines anymore—it was about feeling respected.

That's the power of active listening: it turns complaints into conversations, and conversations into connection.

To develop this skill, try these three core practices:

1. **Reflective Listening** – After someone shares a concern or idea, restate it in your own words. For example: *"So what I'm hearing is that the shift in priorities caught you off guard?"*

2. **Pause Before You Reply** – Give a beat of silence. It shows respect and lets their words land.

3. **Notice What's Not Said** – Watch body language, tone, hesitation. Sometimes, the truth is between the lines.

When leaders like Alex applied this in high-stress meetings, he noticed fewer misunderstandings and more clarity. At first, it felt awkward not to offer solutions immediately. But over time, his team began opening up more, bringing up challenges earlier, suggesting ideas faster, and thanking him for "actually hearing them out."

And here's the bonus: when people feel truly heard, they stop bracing for judgment. That's when collaboration, innovation, and even accountability take root.

📝 *Active Listening Micro-Challenge*

In your next team 1:1 or meeting, choose one person to focus on fully. As they speak:

- Don't interrupt.

- Summarize what you heard.

- Ask one follow-up question that shows you care about their *experience*, not just the result.

Write down afterward:

- *What did I learn that I might have missed before?*
- *How did they respond when I really listened?*

Active listening is more than a technique—it's a leadership superpower. It builds trust, defuses conflict, and creates space for the kind of dialogue that drives real progress.

Building Genuine Connections with Your Team

Imagine leading a team where everyone is technically aligned but emotionally disconnected. The tasks get done, and deadlines are met, but what about the spark? It's missing. Communication feels transactional, collaboration is surface-level, and motivation comes more from obligation than inspiration. Now, in contrast, with a team where trust runs deep, laughter is genuine, and people feel seen, not just managed. That's the power of authentic connection.

Genuine relationships aren't just nice to have—they're the foundation of a high-performing team. When leaders take time to connect beyond the deliverables, something powerful happens: walls come down. People speak up. They lean in. They stop working *for* you and start working *with* you. It's in these honest, human moments that innovation, resilience, and loyalty begin to flourish.

And the key to it all? Authenticity. When you lead with realness—when your words match your actions and show up not as a polished persona but as a present, imperfect person—you send a message that it's safe for others to do the same. This isn't about oversharing or being everyone's best friend. It's about creating a space where people feel comfortable expressing themselves, taking risks, and trusting your leadership—even when things get hard.

Creating genuine connections starts with taking time to know your team members beyond their job titles. One-on-one meetings are pivotal here. They offer a chance to understand individual aspirations, challenges, and motivations. In these meetings, listen more than you speak. Show interest in their lives and goals. This isn't about prying but about showing you care. It's about making your team feel valued and understood.

Shared experiences can also be a powerful tool for building bonds. Team-building activities allow people to connect personally  through a simple lunch or a more structured retreat. These experiences create shared stories and inside jokes that foster camaraderie. It's like adding pieces to a puzzle that eventually forms a picture of unity.

Emotional intelligence plays a crucial role in building relationships. It serves as the bridge that turns casual acquaintances into strong connections. Empathizing with your team lets you gain insights into their emotions and needs. This understanding helps you tailor your leadership approach to each individual, making interactions more meaningful.

The benefits of genuine connections are vast. Enhanced collaboration is one of the most significant outcomes. When people trust each other, they're more likely to collaborate effectively. They share ideas freely, knowing they won't be judged or dismissed. This openness leads to innovative solutions and increased productivity.

Genuine connections also improve team cohesion. When team members feel connected to each other and their leader, they're more committed to collective goals. They work together seamlessly, navigating challenges with ease. This cohesion builds resilience within the team, allowing them to weather storms together without falling apart.

Strong leader-team relationships also lead to higher job satisfaction and reduced turnover rates. When people feel valued and understood, they're more likely to stay loyal to their organization. This loyalty translates into lower attrition rates, saving time and resources spent on recruitment.

So, as you navigate your leadership role, remember that building genuine connections isn't about grand gestures or complex strategies. It's about being present, showing empathy, and fostering an environment where everyone feels valued. It's about understanding that leadership is as much about people as it is about processes. Focusing on these connections will pave the way for a thriving team ready to tackle any challenge together.

As you strengthen these connections, you'll notice subtle shifts in how your team interacts and collaborates. You'll witness increased energy and enthusiasm as people come together with shared purpose and understanding. This transformation won't happen overnight, but with patience and consistency, you'll cultivate an environment where genuine connections flourish, leading to lasting success for you and your team.

Remember that leadership is not just about achieving goals; it's about inspiring others to reach their potential while creating meaningful relationships. By investing in genuine connections with your team, you become more than just a leader; you become a catalyst for growth and collaboration in an organization where everyone thrives together.

Bridging the Empathy Gap: Connecting with Your Team

Leaders often face what's called the empathy gap. This gap represents a disconnect in emotional understanding between leaders and their teams. It's like trying to tune into a radio station but only getting static. When leaders misinterpret or overlook the emotions of their team members, the result is often misalignment, leading to misunderstandings and decreased morale. This disconnect can breed resentment or apathy, causing once-motivated teams to lose their spark.

Bridging this gap requires conscious effort and intention. As stated earlier in this chapter, active listening is essential to this effort. **Empathy-building** exercises also play a vital role. Leaders can engage in activities designed to enhance their ability to understand and share the feelings of others. Simple exercises like role-playing or walking in someone else's shoes can be illuminating. This practice enhances empathy and builds a culture where diverse viewpoints are acknowledged and valued.

Developing empathy isn't a one-time endeavor. It requires continuous nurturing and growth. **You should stay alert, consistently evaluate your empathy, and request feedback from your team.** This ongoing development ensures that empathy becomes an integral part of your leadership style rather than a superficial exercise. Long-term, empathy cultivates resilience within teams, allowing them to weather challenges with unity and understanding.

The journey towards empathetic leadership is ongoing, filled with challenges and triumphs. Yet, as leaders strive to bridge the empathy gap, they open doors to deeper connections and more fulfilling professional relationships. In doing so, they not only enhance their leadership capabilities but also transform the very fabric of their workplace into one of trust and collaboration.

Empathy-in-Action: Your Team Connection Map

This simple reflection exercise will help you tune into your team's emotional state and take one meaningful step toward bridging the empathy gap.

- *Step 1*: **Identify Key Team Members**

List 3–5 people you interact with regularly at work. These could be direct reports, colleagues, or cross-functional collaborators.

- *Step 2*: **Reflect on Each Person**

For each person, answer the following questions:
  - *What do I think they care most about in their role?*
  - *Have I noticed any recent signs of stress or disengagement?*
  - *When was our last meaningful, non-task-related conversation?*
  - *Do I believe they feel safe giving me honest feedback? Why?*

- <u>*Step 3*</u>: **Take Intentional Action**

Choose one person from your list and schedule a brief, informal check-in this week—no agenda, just connection. Ask how they're doing and what support they might need.

- <u>*Step 4*</u>: **Reflect**

After the conversation, take a few minutes to jot down:

- *What did you learn about them that you didn't know before?*
- *How did the conversation feel for you and them?*
- *What could you do differently in the future to maintain a stronger emotional connection?*

Communicating with Clarity and Empathy

We've all been there—delivering what we *thought* was a clear message, only to realize days later that half the team interpreted it five different ways. In fast-paced environments, communication can get noisy fast. It's not just what you say—it's about how clearly, consistently, and compassionately you express yourself. Clear communication keeps the work moving in the right direction. When you articulate your thoughts clearly, you reduce confusion, ensure everyone is on the same page, and steer your team toward shared goals with precision. Like a well-tuned orchestra, clear communication ensures each member knows their part and plays it in harmony.

But clarity without empathy? That's just direction without connection. Pair them, and you've got the kind of communication that doesn't just instruct—it inspires. Empathetic communication acknowledges emotions while conveying your message. It says, "I see you," before saying, "Here's what we need to do."

Sarah learned this the hard way during a high-stakes launch week. Tensions were running high, her team was behind schedule, and everyone was working long hours. During a late-night review, she noticed her developer, Luis, had missed a key update… again.

She was ready to snap—until she caught herself. Instead of leading with frustration, she paused and said, "Luis, I know this week's been intense. Can you walk me through what's been getting in the way?"

Luis looked up, surprised. "Honestly? I've been trying to finish my part while helping the junior developers who are still lost in the new framework."

That moment shifted everything.

Instead of criticizing, Sarah said, "Thanks for stepping up for the team. Let's figure out how to get you the support you need so you're not burning out."

Clarity? She got the update on the radar. Empathy? She acknowledged the effort behind the missed task. That exchange didn't just solve a technical problem—it strengthened trust. Luis wasn't just another engineer—he was seen. That's the power of clarity wrapped in empathy.

Feedback as a Tool for Growth and Connection

Hearing the word "feedback" can make your stomach tight, right? Feedback can feel like a tightrope walk, whether you're giving or receiving it. But here's the truth: when used with intention, feedback is one of the most powerful tools in your leadership arsenal—not for correction but for connection.

Think of feedback as a mirror and a map. It helps someone see how they're showing up and gives them a more straightforward path to where they want to go. It's not about pointing out what's wrong—it's about showing someone what's *possible*. When done right, feedback fuels growth, boosts motivation, and opens the door for meaningful progress for individuals and teams.

To make your feedback land with purpose (instead of resistance), here are a few approaches that work:

- **Start with intention.** Before diving in, ask yourself: *What outcome do I hope for?* If your goal is to help someone grow, that mindset will shape your tone and words.

- **Be specific and actionable.** Instead of saying, "You need to be better in meetings," try, "In today's meeting, I noticed you didn't get a chance to share your ideas. I'd love to hear your input earlier next time—your perspective helps the team."

- **Use the sandwich technique with care.** Starting with something positive, delivering your constructive point, and ending with encouragement can soften the impact, but don't let it dilute your message. It's not about sugarcoating; it's about being kind and clear at the same time.

And here's the part we often forget: *receiving* feedback is just as important as giving it.

The next time someone offers you feedback, especially the uncomfortable kind, pause. Breathe. Then choose curiosity over defensiveness. Ask follow-up questions. Reflect, even if your first reaction is resistance. When you handle feedback openly, you're modeling emotional intelligence and building trust. Your team sees that you're not above growth, which permits them to grow, too.

Think about the ripple effect this can create.

Something powerful happens when feedback becomes part of how your team operates—not a rare event, but a regular rhythm. People become more agile. Innovation increases. People take smart risks because they know they'll get guidance, not judgment, if they miss the mark.

Here's a real-world example: Sarah regularly made feedback part of her sprint reviews. She didn't wait for problems to build up. Instead, she used these moments to highlight wins *and* ask, "What could we do better next time?" Her team didn't just meet deadlines—they grew stronger after every project. They started coming to her with ideas, not just updates. Feedback was a source of energy, not fear.

Meanwhile, when Alex received feedback from his analysts about communication gaps, he didn't get defensive. He listened, reflected, and adjusted. That moment alone deepened the team's trust in his leadership. They saw him not just as a decision-maker but as someone who *walked the talk* of growth.

📝 *Feedback-in-Action: A Simple Leadership Exercise*

Try this in your next one-on-one:

1. **Ask for feedback first.** Start with:

    "What's one thing I could do better to support you right now?"

2. **Listen without interrupting.** Even if it stings, take it in fully.

3. **Acknowledge and reflect.** You don't have to fix it on the spot, but say:
    "Thanks for sharing that—I'm going to think more about it and see where I can adjust."

4. **Offer feedback in return.** Use this structure:

    o   One thing you appreciate

    o   One area to grow

    o   One suggestion to move forward

Feedback isn't about being "nice" or "tough." It's about being clear, caring, and committed to helping people thrive. And when you lead that way, you don't just build skills—you build a culture of courage, trust, and continuous growth.

Enhancing Team Dynamics through Emotional Intelligence

Team dynamics are the invisible threads that shape how a group communicates, collaborates, and responds to pressure. When those threads are tangled through unspoken tension, unclear expectations, or mismatched energy, things start to break down, even if performance metrics look fine on paper. But when those threads are strong, everything changes. A team doesn't just function—it flows. Ideas move freely, conflict becomes constructive, and people actually enjoy solving problems together.

This transformation doesn't require a complete team overhaul or a flashy offsite. It starts with emotional intelligence. When a leader learns to notice emotional undercurrents—hesitation in someone's tone, a sudden dip in enthusiasm, the way two teammates stop sitting next to each other—it opens the door to real understanding. And from that understanding comes action.

Take Sarah, for example. She began to sense that one of her senior developers was withdrawing. Nothing obvious—just fewer contributions in meetings and quick replies to Slack. Instead of brushing it off or waiting for HR to step in, she initiated a check-in. It is not a formal performance review—just a genuine one. "How have you been feeling about the work lately?" That one question led to a transformative discussion about burnout, priorities, and the need for more creative input. They made a few simple adjustments to his role, and within weeks, his energy returned. So did his ideas.

Alex had a similar breakthrough. During a period of restructuring, his team grew quiet and hesitant. Instead of assuming everything was fine—or worse, demanding more enthusiasm, he named what he sensed. "There's a heaviness lately," he told them during a team huddle. "If there's something we're not saying, I'd rather talk about it now than let it keep building." The response was immediate. People opened up about uncertainty, fear of being left behind, and even tension with other departments. That conversation didn't solve everything overnight, but restored one crucial element: trust. And with trust back on the table, solutions followed.

This is what emotional intelligence does—it gives leaders the tools to tune in, speak up, and respond with intention. It turns unspoken friction into productive dialogue and transforms isolated work into shared purpose. Teams begin to feel like communities, not just collections of employees. And when people feel safe and valued, they don't just do good work—they bring their best work forward.

Enhancing team dynamics is not about being the most charismatic person in the room. It's about being emotionally present. It's about asking how someone's doing—and meaning it. It's about noticing when something feels off and being willing to address it with compassion, not control.

And the payoff? It's powerful. Teams with strong dynamics move faster, think deeper, and support each other through challenges. They adapt instead of resisting. They engage instead of withdrawing. And they grow together.

As we wrap this chapter on interpersonal skills and communication,

take a moment to reflect on your own team. What energy are you walking into each day? What might be unsaid that's quietly shaping how your team functions? Because here's the truth: emotional intelligence doesn't just help you *lead* better—it helps your team *live* better at work.

In the next chapter, we'll dive deeper into one of the most challenging aspects of leadership: conflict. Conflict is inevitable, whether it's between team members, across departments, or within yourself. But when approached with emotional intelligence, it doesn't have to divide—it can unite. You'll learn to turn disagreements into breakthroughs and hold your ground without losing empathy.

Let's keep going. The real leadership growth is just getting started.

TOP 3 TAKEAWAYS
(CHAPTER 4)

1   Listening is your leadership litmus test.

Most people hear to reply — real leaders listen to *understand.* When you pause, reflect, and respond with presence, you turn surface conversations into trust-building moments. Connection starts when your team feels truly seen and heard.

2   Empathy builds more than rapport — it builds culture.

Authentic connection isn't a leadership extra; it's the foundation of team resilience. When you lead with emotional honesty and curiosity, you close the empathy gap, defuse tension, and spark collaboration that goes deeper than checklists.

3   Clarity plus care equals communication that moves people.

Words matter. But tone, timing, and intention matter more. When you combine direct feedback with emotional intelligence, you don't just manage performance — you unlock potential and create a safe space where people grow, speak up, and stay.

Pause and Reflect
Your Growth Is Worth Sharing

You've now explored meaningful concepts about emotional intelligence, self-awareness, and leading with heart.

What insight has shifted your perspective?

What story or skill has stayed with you?

Take a moment to jot down a personal reflection or share your favorite takeaway online. Your voice not only reflects your journey; it also helps other leaders grow.

Whether you're new to leadership or seasoned in your role, your experience is a spark that can inspire someone else to lead with greater empathy and courage.

Let's maintain this ripple effect—one insight at a time.

Chapter 5: Conflict Resolution and Team Cohesion

"You can't stop the waves, but you can learn to surf."
— Jon Kabat-Zinn

If leadership had a 'fine print,' it would read: must be willing to have awkward, emotional, high-stakes conversations—and handle them with grace. These discussions frequently focus on delicate topics, including performance issues, layoffs, or interpersonal conflicts. They're challenging because they tap into the emotional reservoirs of both parties, making it easy for discussions to spiral into misunderstandings or defensiveness. As a leader, your role is to guide these conversations with a steady hand, keeping them productive rather than adversarial.

Preparation is your ally in navigating these tricky waters. Before diving into a conversation, take a moment to set clear intentions. Know what you want to achieve and anticipate possible emotional responses. This foresight will help you steer the dialogue toward a constructive outcome. It's akin to planning a journey; you wouldn't embark without a map, so why enter a discussion without clarity? Additionally, creating a safe environment for dialogue is crucial. Choose a neutral space where both parties can speak freely without feeling threatened. This setting fosters openness and trust, laying the groundwork for a meaningful exchange.

Emotional intelligence is your compass when emotions run high during difficult conversations. It equips you with the tools to regulate your own feelings and respond to others with empathy and understanding. Imagine being caught in a heated exchange, your instincts urging you to react defensively. Instead, emotional intelligence allows you to pause, take a deep breath, and respond thoughtfully.

Alex recently had to address performance concerns with a rising star on his team—a young analyst who had missed several deadlines over the past quarter. Before the meeting, Alex reviewed the data and identified patterns, but he also reflected on his goal: to support the analyst's development, not just point out mistakes. Alex began the conversation with empathy when they sat down: "I've noticed some delays recently, and I wanted to check in—not just about the work, but how you're doing overall." As the discussion unfolded, the analyst admitted to struggling with time management and feeling overwhelmed but too embarrassed to ask for help. Rather than criticizing, Alex acknowledged the vulnerability, affirmed their value to the team, and co-created a plan to rebuild structure and confidence. What could've been a demoralizing critique turned into a moment of empowerment—and a turning point in their working relationship.

Meanwhile, Sarah was in a brewing conflict between her lead developer and product manager. Tension had been mounting over shifting deadlines and unclear scope, and their latest disagreement had left the team fragmented. Rather than let frustration fester, Sarah brought both team members together for a conversation. She opened with a reminder of shared goals and ground rules for respectful dialogue, then asked each person to share their perspective, without interruption. As emotions surfaced, Sarah stayed steady. She reflected back on what she had heard, acknowledged frustrations on both sides, and helped them identify the real issue: a misalignment in communication, not competence or intent. With patience and empathy, she guided them toward a shared solution. The result? The immediate conflict was resolved, and the two began collaborating more proactively. They are now aligned by mutual respect and a leader who showed them how to navigate tension with clarity and care.

Checklist for Preparing Difficult Conversations

Difficult conversations aren't detours—they're the direct path to growth, trust, and resolution. And like any tough conversation, they go better when you show up with clarity, compassion, and a plan. Below is a step-by-step checklist to help you prepare with confidence and emotional intelligence.

➢ *Step 1*: **Clarify Your Purpose**

Before you say a word, ask yourself:
- *What outcome am I hoping for?*
- *Is this about correction, clarification, or collaboration?*

Example: Before addressing a team member's missed deadlines, Sarah took a moment to define her goal: not to reprimand, but to understand what's getting in the way and to offer support. That clarity shaped her tone and approach.

➢ *Step 2*: **Choose the Right Setting**

The environment matters. Select a neutral, private space where both of you can speak openly—there will be no looming audience and no distractions.

Tip: A quiet conference room is better than your office, where power dynamics might feel intensified.

> ***Step 3***: **Regulate Your Emotions**

Don't bring nervous energy or frustration into the room. Instead, ground yourself beforehand using tools like:
• Deep breathing
• Visualization (picture the conversation going calmly and well)
• Brief journaling to clear emotional clutter

Think of this as your pre-conversation warm-up.

> ***Step 4***: **Anticipate Emotional Responses**

Put yourself in their shoes:
• *How might they feel hearing this feedback?*
• *What might trigger defensiveness?*
• *Where can empathy guide your words?*

Example: When Alex prepared to discuss role adjustments with a senior analyst, he anticipated resistance—and planned affirming statements to ease the tension, like: *"This change isn't about questioning your value—it's about realigning responsibilities to match team goals."*

> ***Step 5***: **Practice Active Listening**

Once the conversation begins, your primary role isn't just to speak—it's to listen.
• Reflect what you hear: *"So what I'm hearing is..."*
• Validate emotions, even if you disagree with the perspective
• Keep your body language open and attentive

➢ *Step 6*: **End with a Forward Step**

Even the most challenging conversations should leave both parties with a clear next step.
- *What's the plan going forward?*
- *What support will you offer?*
- *When will you follow up?*

When handled with emotional intelligence, difficult conversations become leadership milestones. They demonstrate your commitment not just to outcomes, but to people. They strengthen trust, sharpen clarity, and create space for accountability without blame.

The more you practice this process, the more your confidence will grow. These conversations won't always feel easy, but they will start to feel purposeful, productive, and real.

And that's where true leadership happens.

Root Causes of Workplace Conflicts

> *"Tension doesn't knock. It creeps in quietly—and if you're not paying attention, it takes over."*

Picture this: it's a calm morning, and you're settling into your day with a warm coffee. But then, something shifts. A strained voice, an unusually quiet cubicle, a lingering silence after a team stand-up. You can't quite put your finger on it, but you feel it—something's off.

Workplace conflict rarely announces itself. Like the sour scent of spoiled milk, the signs are subtle initially—until they're not. If left unaddressed, those quiet rumbles become full-blown earthquakes that shake trust, stall momentum, and corrode team morale.

Sarah once described it as "feeling the tension before anyone names it." For Alex, it showed up in skipped lunches and unread Slack messages—small cues that something deeper was brewing.

So, what causes these workplace undercurrents? Let's unpack the usual suspects:

1. Personality Clashes

Imagine two vibrant, patterned socks—each bold in its own way, but completely mismatched together. That's what happens when strong personalities collide. Differences in communication styles, work ethics, or core values can spark friction, especially in high-pressure environments. One person thrives on speed; another values precision. Without awareness, what starts as a difference can become a disconnect.

2. Miscommunication

Ever played a game of telephone? What begins as a clear message transforms into something completely different when it reaches the last person. That's miscommunication at work—emails misinterpreted, feedback taken the wrong way, or unclear expectations that spiral into resentment. The irony? Everyone might think they're on the same page—until they're not.

3. Resource Competition

Think musical chairs—but the stakes are deadlines, budget, and recognition. When there's not enough time, support, or visibility to go around, even the most collaborative teams can slip into competition mode. This scarcity mindset creates tension, fuels frustration, and fractures trust.

What Happens When Conflicts Are Ignored?

Picture baking a cake without mixing the ingredients. It may appear fine on the outside, but after one slice, it crumbles. Teams can be the same. On the surface, everything seems to function, but underneath, unresolved tension simmers. Morale drops, engagement wanes, and productivity suffers.

Sarah learned to recognize subtle cues: the colleague who suddenly stopped volunteering in meetings, the tight-lipped silence after feedback. Alex started noticing tone shifts in emails and the way people responded to calendar invites—tiny breadcrumbs that something needed attention.

Emotional intelligence is like a sixth sense. It helps you read the room beyond words—decoding body language, tone, and energy before conflict boils over.

Here's how emotionally intelligent leaders stay ahead of conflict:

- **Regular check-ins**: Think of them like car maintenance. Quick chats, casual coffee talks, or structured one-on-ones are a chance to catch concerns early.

- **Open feedback channels**: Like pressure-release valves, they offer your team a safe outlet to express frustration before it explodes.

- **Emotional scanning**: Observing energy levels, tone shifts, or even someone's withdrawal can help you intervene with care before things unravel.

📄 *Conflict Detection Checklist*

Use this reflection tool to sharpen your conflict radar:

☐ Have I noticed shifts in tone, body language, or participation in meetings?

☐ Am I holding regular one-on-ones where honesty feels safe?

☐ Are there recurring complaints or interpersonal patterns I've overlooked?

☐ Have I invited feedback on resource fairness or workload balance?

Don't just run through the list—live with it. Observe, listen, and trust your intuition. Often, the best leaders catch a conflict not because someone raised a flag, but because they noticed a whisper.

When you lead with emotional awareness, you become the leader people trust to keep the air clear, even when things get stormy. Identifying the root causes of conflict and addressing them early protects your team's cohesion, restores momentum, and creates space for genuine connection and innovation to thrive.

Great teams aren't built by avoiding conflict but by navigating it with courage, clarity, and emotional depth.

Conflict Resolution Strategies for Leaders

"It's not about who's right—it's about what's next."

When conflict surfaces, it's not a sign that something's broken—it's a signal that something deeper needs attention. And as a leader, your response doesn't just fix the issue. It teaches your team how safe it is to disagree—and how powerful it is to resolve.

One of the most effective approaches? *Collaborative problem-solving.* It's not about being the smartest person in the room—it's about being the connector. The leader who knows that different perspectives aren't obstacles to a solution—they *are* the solution. Think of it like rebuilding a bridge from both sides of the river. The stronger the materials—trust, clarity, empathy—the faster the crossing.

Sarah learned this on the second day as her senior engineers nearly derailed a sprint over competing tech stacks. Instead of choosing sides, she called a timeout. Brought them both into a whiteboard session. Asked questions, not for drama, but for understanding: "What are you trying to protect? What would success look like from your view?" Within an hour, the tone had shifted from battle to blueprint. By the end of the week, they had co-designed a hybrid solution and a newfound respect for each other's approach.

Now, compromise isn't always romantic. It's not about singing "Kumbaya" and splitting everything down the middle. It's about knowing which hills matter and which ones are just your ego in disguise. Great leaders know when to negotiate, not out of weakness, but from wisdom. They give a little to gain a lot, like

Alex, who once mediated a budget tug-of-war between marketing and engineering by proposing a joint pilot project. Both departments kept partial funding, and the collaboration unexpectedly birthed a campaign that went viral. Everyone won. Because the goal wasn't to "win." It was to move forward.

But let's be clear—none of this works without emotional intelligence. EQ is what separates a resolution from a temporary ceasefire. It's what helps you hear what's *not* being said. That long pause. That clipped email. That team member who hasn't spoken up in weeks.

It's what helped Alex navigate one of the trickiest conflicts of his career—a rising analyst clashing with a veteran manager. Tensions were high, and neither party was backing down. But instead of jumping in with solutions, Alex slowed it down. He met with each person individually, listened—really listened—and asked: "What's at stake for you here?" By the time they met together, the air had cleared. The conversation wasn't about ego anymore—it was about expectations. Boundaries were redefined. Feedback channels were rebuilt. And trust? It didn't just recover—it deepened.

Neutrality is key during moments like these. A leader's job in conflict isn't to play judge. It's to hold the space where honesty can happen without retaliation. Where people can bring their messy truths and still feel safe. That requires tone. Posture. Language. You don't say, "You didn't deliver." You say, "Help me understand what got in the way." You don't say, "We can't afford mistakes like this." You say, "Let's look at what we missed and how we can learn from it."

Conflict handled with care becomes a connection. But conflict dodged? That becomes decay. Slowly, quietly, teams fracture—not because they're not talented, but because no one dared to talk about the tension.

That's why creating a culture of collaboration isn't a nice-to-have—it's non-negotiable. And it doesn't start with trust falls or off-sites. It begins with the mundane. How you manage disagreement. How you celebrate disagreement. How you create a safe space to say, "I see it differently."

Sarah and Alex began encouraging cross-functional micro-projects—quick wins where marketing, tech, and finance could co-create, not just to build deliverables but also relationships. Over time, friction faded. Confidence grew. People weren't just rowing harder—they were rowing together.

And when it came time for tough negotiations—whether deadline extensions or resource reallocations—they had the muscle memory. Teams knew how to listen, compromise, and stay anchored in shared goals.

Because that's the secret to high-functioning teams: not avoiding conflict, but being exceptional at navigating through it.

So, the next time a disagreement arises, ask yourself: Not, *Who's right?* But, *What's the next right step for the team?*

And then lead like you mean it—steady, clear, and emotionally present. The kind of leader who doesn't just fix conflict, but transforms it into momentum.

Building Trust and Credibility through Conflict Resolution

> *"It's not how you handle the easy days that builds your reputation—it's how you navigate the hard ones."*

Every leader wants to be trusted. But trust doesn't just show up because you hold a title. It's built moment by moment, especially when the stakes are high and the tension is real. And one of the most powerful (and overlooked) places to earn that trust? Conflict.

When handled consistently and transparently, conflict resolution becomes your leadership calling card. It tells your team, "You can count on me, even when things get uncomfortable."

Think of it like muscle memory. If your team sees that you handle tension with fairness, not favoritism, and presence, not panic, they start to relax. They know the rules aren't shifting with the wind. That reliability becomes your brand.

Alex once inherited a team known for internal silos and finger-pointing. The first conflict he mediated was small—a disagreement over task ownership—but how he handled it set the tone. He didn't sweep it under the rug or take sides. He brought the team together, clarified the friction, and walked through the resolution step-by-step in front of everyone. The message was clear: "We don't avoid tension. We resolve it—together." That decision changed how the team showed up for the rest of the quarter.

Transparency matters. People trust you more when they understand how you make decisions, not just what you decide. Think of it like pulling back the curtain. Instead of playing the wise wizard behind a mysterious screen, you walk your team through your thinking. You involve them. You listen. You explain the why. And that clarity builds credibility.

Sarah learned this during a high-pressure launch when budget constraints forced her to reassign resources mid-sprint. She could've delivered the decision as a done deal. Instead, she gathered the team, shared the full context, and invited their input on what to deprioritize. Some were frustrated, but all of them felt respected. And when the project succeeded, it wasn't just a technical win—it was a trust milestone.

Here's what happens when you lead this way: Your team stops walking on eggshells. They start taking healthy risks. They speak up earlier. They lean in. Because they know that if conflict arises, it won't be met with punishment—it'll be met with process and presence.

Conflict resolution becomes less about *putting out fires* and more about *laying foundations*. Each resolution is a quiet brick in the trust you're building—a reputation for being steady, fair, and human.

And that kind of trust? It doesn't just boost morale. It supercharges performance. Teams aligned by trust move faster, think more creatively, and stay resilient in the face of setbacks. They're not just rowing harder—they're rowing *together*.

But let's be clear: trust isn't built in a single moment. It's built in every moment you choose calm over chaos, clarity over confusion, and empathy over ego. It's not a speech. It's a pattern. And over time, that pattern becomes your leadership legacy.

So next time conflict shows up—and it will—ask yourself:

- *Am I being consistent?*
- *Am I being transparent?*
- *Am I modeling what I want repeated?*

Because trust isn't earned when it's easy, it's earned when things get real.

Emotional Intelligence in Negotiation and Mediation

> *"Some leaders negotiate for control. Emotionally intelligent ones negotiate for connection."*

Let's drop you into a moment that every leader dreads—but must master: a high-stakes negotiation. The tension is almost tangible. Words are measured. Silence feels strategic. Every participant sits at the edge of their priorities, determined not to blink first.

Now pause.

This is where most people lean on strategy. But the best leaders? They reach for emotional intelligence. Because the real work isn't happening in the words being spoken—it's in the pauses between them. The furrowed brow. The clipped tone. The eye contact that lingers just a beat too long. These aren't distractions. They're data. And if you're paying attention, they'll tell you everything.

Sarah once walked into a vendor negotiation where both parties had their heels dug in. On paper, the two sides were gridlocked. But instead of forcing compromise with corporate jargon and bullet-pointed decks, she read the room. She noticed the tension wasn't about deadlines or pricing—it was about trust. So, she asked one simple question: "What are you most worried about if we move forward?" That broke the dam. Suddenly, both sides stopped posturing and started problem-solving. Not because she "won"—but because she listened.

That's the core of emotionally intelligent negotiation: tuning into the *emotional current* so you can navigate what logic alone can't solve.

It starts with active listening—not the kind where you're just waiting for your turn to talk, but the kind that makes the other person feel like they *matter*. Real listening is disarming. When someone feels truly heard, their defenses lower, their reasoning expands, and their willingness to collaborate grows. It's less about tactics and more about presence.

Alex once mediated a heated budget dispute between two department leads. His first instinct was to split the resources evenly. Fair, right? But instead, he set that aside and asked each person to explain what was *really* at stake for their team. One spoke about retention issues; the other, a looming product launch. Different needs. Different pressures. With that clarity, they didn't just negotiate—they co-created a solution. One that addressed urgency without ignoring long-term impact. That shift—listening first, deciding second—turned a tense standoff into an unexpected alliance.

When emotions get heated, as they often do, emotional self-regulation becomes your secret sauce. In the middle of a tough discussion, the person with the calmest tone holds the most power, not because they dominate, but because they *stabilize*. You become the anchor in the chaos, the one who makes it safe for others to express themselves without fear of retaliation or judgment.

This kind of calm leadership doesn't silence emotion—it *holds* it. It tells the room: "We can disagree without tearing each other apart." That's how you turn a mediation from a battleground into common ground.

And here's where it gets beautiful: mediation isn't about one side winning. It's about both sides walking away feeling respected. Picture it less like a debate and more like a dance. You're not trying to overpower your partner—you're trying to stay in rhythm, to find that shared beat where collaboration can happen.

Take deadline negotiations, for example. Instead of pushing a date with brute logic, imagine saying: "I know how much pressure you're under. What would it take to make this timeline feel realistic—*and* keep quality intact?" That's not softness. That's leadership with spine and soul.

And when you consistently lead this way and approach tough conversations with empathy, curiosity, and calm, you don't just resolve conflict. You build something bigger: trust.

That trust becomes currency. It pays off when future negotiations arise, teams are stretched thin, and new fires pop up. People remember how you made them feel *in the hard moments*. That's the difference between compliance and commitment.

So no, emotional intelligence isn't a "nice to have" in negotiations—it's your sharpest tool. The one that helps you *see* beneath the surface, *connect* across perspectives, and *create* outcomes that don't just work, but *last*.

Real leadership isn't about negotiating louder.

It's about negotiating *wiser*.

Creating a Culture of Open Communication

> *"Great leaders don't just encourage openness—*
> *they embody it."*

Open communication isn't just a leadership skill—it's the ecosystem where trust, innovation, and collaboration breathe freely. When honesty isn't just allowed but *expected*, teams stop playing defense and start playing to win.

At its core, open communication is about creating a space where people feel safe to speak up—whether sharing a new idea, surfacing a concern, or offering feedback that might be uncomfortable. It's a culture where people don't wonder if their voice matters—they know it does.

Sarah experienced this transformation firsthand. Early in her leadership, she ran efficient meetings—tight, focused, controlled. But something was off. Her team left those meetings informed... but disengaged. Everything changed when she began pausing for open-ended questions, making space for silent voices, and welcoming disagreement as a form of engagement. The conversations deepened. The ideas got sharper. And the team leaned in—because the table finally had room for *them*.

Building this kind of culture takes more than intention—it takes consistency. It means turning team meetings into *honest dialogue*, not just status updates. Instead of "Any questions?" try:

- *"What's missing from this plan?"*
- *"What do you see that I might not?"*

Questions like these don't just invite feedback—they normalize it.

Then there's the open door—not just physically, but emotionally. When leaders are approachable, available, and responsive, communication doesn't get bottlenecked by hierarchy. It flows. And that openness becomes a release valve when something goes sideways (as it always does). Issues get surfaced early. Minor conflicts don't metastasize into team dysfunction. Leaders who stay close to the pulse of their people don't just manage—they lead with clarity.

Alex found this out during a period of heavy transition. Rumors were swirling. Morale was dipping. Instead of locking himself away to finalize new plans, he called a series of team huddles and said, "Here's what we know. Here's what we don't. Here's how you can help shape what happens next." That moment of transparency didn't solve every problem, but it stopped the speculation cold.

That's the thing about open communication—it's not fluffy. It's foundational. It prevents conflicts before they ignite, builds psychological safety, and transforms feedback from a risk into a ritual.

When communication flows freely, something powerful happens: people start thinking bigger and taking bolder action. They don't just follow—they contribute, create, and lead from wherever they are.

As we close this chapter on conflict resolution and team cohesion, one truth becomes clear: *open communication is the heartbeat of high-performing teams.* Without it, even the best intentions falter. With it, trust deepens, missteps are corrected early, and collaboration becomes not just possible but inevitable.

And this leads us to our next step.

In the following chapter, we'll explore how emotional intelligence enhances leaders' decision-making. When communication flows and trust is established, leaders are better equipped to weigh data and its emotional context. This intersection of clarity and empathy is where wise, inclusive, and high-impact decisions are made.

Because communication opens the door.

Emotional intelligence walks us through it.

TOP 3 TAKEAWAYS
(CHAPTER 5)

1 Conflict isn't chaos—it's a doorway to clarity.

When handled with emotional intelligence, conflict stops being something to avoid and becomes a chance to build trust, reset expectations, and strengthen relationships. Great leaders don't dodge tension; they navigate it with courage and calm.

2 How you handle hard conversations defines your leadership.

Anyone can lead on easy days. Real credibility is built when stakes are high and emotions are hot, whether it's giving tough feedback or mediating friction, your tone, presence, and consistency shape how safe your team feels speaking up.

3 Communication isn't just a tool—it's your culture.

Open dialogue is the heartbeat of a healthy team. When people know they can share ideas, raise concerns, and challenge decisions without fear, collaboration thrives, resilience grows, and momentum follows. That kind of openness isn't a suggestion—it's a leadership standard.

Chapter 6: Building Trust Through Cultural Competence

"Diversity is being invited to the party; inclusion is being asked to dance." — Verna Myers

Diversity in teams isn't a buzzword—it's a strategic advantage. But only if you know how to use it.

When people from different cultures, languages, and backgrounds come together, they bring more than their skills. They bring unspoken values, nuanced communication styles, and emotional wiring shaped by lived experience. In this space, emotional intelligence becomes your most powerful leadership asset—not a soft skill but a critical connector.

It helps you see beyond the surface of silence or enthusiasm and understand what isn't said.

Consider a moment when a team member stays quiet in a group discussion. To some leaders, silence reads as disengagement or discomfort. But emotional intelligence invites a better question: What might this silence mean in their cultural context? For some, it's respect. For others, it's caution. For still others, it's strategic listening. The emotionally intelligent leader doesn't rush to interpret—they pause, observe, and adapt.

Diverse teams—when led with emotional intelligence—don't just solve problems. They reinvent them. The mix of perspectives challenges assumptions, reveals blind spots, and uncovers unconventional ideas. Innovation doesn't just come from creativity; it comes from contrast. And contrast, handled without empathy, turns into friction. But handled with empathy? It becomes fuel.

Still, the path isn't always smooth. Misunderstandings are inevitable when multiple languages, cultural references, or communication norms are involved. A phrase that motivates one team member might confuse or offend another. A direct email might feel efficient to some and harsh to others.

This is where emotional intelligence earns its place in your toolkit—not in reacting to missteps but in anticipating them. It means listening between the lines, adjusting your tone, asking more, and assuming less. And when conflict arises—as it will—it means approaching it with curiosity, not control.

Alex faced this challenge during a global rollout, when a French designer and a Brazilian analyst clashed over timelines and tone.

What began as a disagreement about deliverables quickly revealed deeper cultural gaps: one prized clarity, the other favored flexibility. But Alex stepped in as a bridge instead of a referee. He acknowledged both perspectives, facilitated a conversation about expectations, and helped reframe the tension as difference, not disrespect. What could have fractured trust instead deepened it.

Leaders who thrive in multicultural environments don't wait for comfort zones. They create spaces where various voices can be heard, not just the loudest. They host meetings that welcome accent, pace, and pause. They ask questions like:

- *"What's your perspective on this from your point of view?"*
- *"Is this how your team typically works best?"*
- *"What would help you feel fully heard right now?"*

These aren't just good habits. They're powerful signals: You matter here, exactly as you are.

And here's where empathy does its quiet magic. It turns awkward pauses into meaningful space. It replaces judgment with context. And sometimes, it speaks loudest through silence—a nod, a thoughtful wait, a well-timed smile.

Because when words fail, presence speaks.

Reflection Practice: Cultivating Emotional Intelligence Across Cultures

The strongest cross-cultural leaders aren't those who know everything—they're the ones who notice, reflect, and grow. Use this reflection practice to build deeper emotional awareness across cultural contexts.

Each week, journal for 10–15 minutes after a team interaction, project debrief, or meeting involving culturally diverse voices. Don't just document what happened—focus on *how* it felt, what you noticed, and how you responded.

Here are some prompts to guide your reflection:

- Where did I notice cultural differences in today's interaction?
  (Think about silence, tone, feedback styles, body language, etc.)
- How did I adapt—or fail to adapt—my leadership or communication style?
  (Be honest. Growth starts here.)
- What emotion was present in the room, and did I miss or misread any cues?
- Was there a moment I could have shown more empathy or curiosity?
- What did this teach me about myself as a cross-cultural leader?
- What's one shift I can try next time—whether in how I speak, listen, or facilitate dialogue?

Keep this journal as a living document—your roadmap for expanding cultural empathy and emotional intelligence.

Leadership isn't just about what you say—it's about how you notice, adjust, and make people feel *seen*.

The more often you reflect, the more naturally you'll begin to lead with cultural awareness, compassion, and presence—qualities that turn diverse teams into powerful engines of creativity, trust, and transformation.

Developing Cultural Competence as a Leader

Great leaders don't just lead—they translate across cultures.

Cultural competence isn't optional in today's global, hybrid, beautifully complex workplaces. It's your edge. It allows you to genuinely connect, not merely communicate. It empowers and fosters a sense of belonging.

Cultural competence is understanding, appreciating, and working effectively across cultural differences. But let's be clear—it's not about memorizing holidays or greeting customs. It's about showing up with humility, curiosity, and a willingness to be changed by what you learn.

Developing this kind of intelligence takes intention. It's like learning a new language—not the grammar but the rhythm. You start slowly, listen more, stumble, and grow. Over time, what once felt foreign becomes familiar.

A significant first step? Step outside your lens.

Attend cultural fluency workshops. Read beyond your usual scope. Follow thought leaders who challenge your worldview. But don't stop at content—seek out people. Build relationships across differences. Find a mentor from a background unlike yours and ask the questions that start with, *"What have you experienced that I haven't?"*

As a leader, your cultural competence doesn't stay in theory. It shows up in how you hold space for different voices, navigate conflict, and assign opportunities. It shapes whether your team feels safe showing up fully or quietly adapting to survive.

Take Sarah, for example. After her promotion to global product lead, she suddenly managed a remote team across six time zones and five cultures. The first few weeks were rocky—deadlines slipped, meetings felt tense, and feedback was met with awkward silence.

At first, she assumed her usual direct approach wasn't landing because people were disengaged. But after a series of quiet one-on-ones, she discovered something deeper: her Brazilian team member saw deadlines as flexible guidelines, not immovable targets. Her Japanese engineer viewed speaking up in meetings as disrespectful unless asked directly. And her German designer preferred written feedback, not because she disliked conversation, but because she wanted to reflect before responding.

So, Sarah changed.

She staggered meeting times to honor time zones. She followed up discussions with written summaries for those who needed to process. She made space at the start of calls for personal check-ins—a small shift that had a big impact.

The result wasn't just smoother meetings. It was deeper trust, stronger buy-in, and a team that started sharing more boldly—because they finally felt seen, not just managed.

That's the power of applied cultural competence: it removes friction before it starts. And it doesn't just create better collaboration—it unlocks innovation. Because when you bring together people who think differently, and make them feel seen, brilliant things happen.

Satya Nadella's leadership at Microsoft offers a powerful example. When he took the helm, he didn't just shift strategy—he shifted mindset. His empathy-forward, inclusion-driven approach transformed a rigid tech culture into one that values learning over knowing. By elevating diverse voices, he fueled both engagement and breakthrough thinking.

And that's the goal—not perfection, but presence. Not performance, but progress.

You won't always get it right. Cultural competence isn't about being fluent in everyone's customs—it's about knowing that customs exist. It's about checking your assumptions at the door and inviting others to do the same. It's about asking, "What am I missing?" and meaning it.

So, start where you are.

Ask yourself:

- Whose voice is missing from this table?
- How might my default leadership style need to stretch?
- What does respect look like—not for me—but for *them*?

Because leadership isn't just about managing outcomes. It's about elevating people. All people.

When you lead with cultural competence, you build better teams that reflect the world we want to live in.

Overcoming Unconscious Bias with Emotional Intelligence

Unconscious bias is a bit like an invisible puppet master, subtly pulling the strings behind our decisions without our knowledge, much like a shadow silently accompanying us, unnoticed but always present. This phenomenon subtly infiltrates the crevices of our thoughts, shaping how we perceive people based on ingrained stereotypes instead of concrete facts or genuine individual traits. In leadership, this silent influencer can lead to skewed decision-making processes, inadvertently restricting team harmony and effectiveness. Picture the hiring or promotion processes; when bias slips in undetected, it alters choices significantly, potentially overlooking remarkable talent and limiting the diversity of thought and experience in favor of more familiar profiles. This isn't just a matter of fairness—it's about the pivotal importance of harnessing the full potential that a diverse workforce brings to the table. By recognizing and diligently addressing these biases, leaders can create more equitable environments that thrive on genuine merit and varied perspectives.

So, where does emotional intelligence come in? Right at the root.

Emotional intelligence doesn't just help you manage teams—it enables you to manage yourself. And when it comes to bias, self-awareness is your entry point. It's the quiet, unflinching skill of noticing your instinct before acting on it. That "gut feeling" about who's a better cultural fit? Pause. That certainty about who's "ready for more"? Rewind. Emotional intelligence allows you to slow the autopilot and ask: *What else could be true?*

During a leadership offsite, Sarah experienced this firsthand, where her team nominated candidates for an upcoming mentorship program. She noticed that every name suggested came from the same vocal, highly visible circle of contributors. She realized her own initial mental shortlist mirrored that bias. So, she did what emotionally intelligent leaders do—she dug deeper. She asked each team lead to reflect on overlooked potential. She opened anonymous submissions. She even initiated one-on-one check-ins to ask quieter team members what support or visibility they'd need to grow.

The outcome wasn't just a more diverse mentorship group but a shift in team culture. Team members began recognizing potential beyond surface-level signals. Bias hadn't just been identified and disarmed through intentional awareness and action.

Tools like bias-awareness training can help uncover blind spots, but pairing them with emotional intelligence practices makes the learning stick. Practices like reflective journaling, 360° feedback, and scenario-based empathy mapping all sharpen your sensitivity to the stories we subconsciously tell ourselves about others.

It's not always comfortable. But that's the point. Growth often hides on the other side of discomfort.

Your team notices when you make the effort. They see when you rethink a snap judgment, when you create space in meetings for less dominant voices, and when you seek input from someone who doesn't always speak first. These micro-movements signal something powerful: *leadership that is learning out loud.*

Emotional intelligence gives leaders the courage and clarity to stop defaulting to the familiar and start choosing the intentional.

Because when unconscious bias is named, it loses its grip. And when leaders lead with awareness, fairness, and empathy, everyone rises.

TOP 3 TAKEAWAYS
(CHAPTER 6)

1   Diversity means nothing without empathy.

Bringing different voices to the table isn't enough — you must *hear* them. Emotional intelligence helps leaders slow down, listen deeper, and honor cultural differences as strategic assets, not communication hurdles.

2   Inclusion isn't accidental; it's intentional.

Inclusive leaders redesign the room, not the people. They shift meeting formats, feedback loops, and decision-making structures so everyone can contribute without code-switching or shrinking themselves to fit in.

3   Cultural competence starts with curiosity, not correctness.

You don't need to be an expert in every background — you must stay open, ask better questions, and adjust when needed. Leadership in diverse teams means learning out loud and letting empathy do the heavy lifting.

Chapter 7: How Emotionally Smart Leaders Rise in Crisis

"In the middle of every difficulty lies opportunity."
— Albert Einstein

Picture this: A large, well-known company is facing a storm of criticism. One of their products has malfunctioned badly, and public outrage is growing louder by the hour. News outlets are circling like hawks, and social media is boiling. People want answers—fast.

Most leaders would panic. Some would hide. Others would point fingers. But not this one.

The CEO steps forward with a strange sense of calm in the hurricane's eye—not the robotic kind that comes from media training but the real kind that comes from knowing who you are and what matters. Their voice doesn't tremble. Their message isn't defensive. They acknowledge the mistake, explain the fix, and offer a sincere apology without trying to spin it.

And something remarkable happens: the anger softens. People begin listening. Some even nod in appreciation. Because what they're seeing isn't just a leader doing damage control. They're witnessing someone who knows how to lead with heart, even when everything around them is falling apart.

Now shift scenes. This time, it's a financial crisis. A major institution is taking a hit. The numbers are plummeting, and tension has overtaken every hallway and meeting room. Employees are walking around with that thousand-yard stare. Everyone's waiting for anyone to say it will be okay.

The chief financial officer doesn't lock themselves away with a calculator and a cup of strong coffee. Instead, they gather the team. They make space for everyone to speak. Not just the usual suspects with titles, but everyone. People share their fears, their frustrations, and their ideas. And the CFO listens—not with that polite, corporate nod, but with full presence. They don't rush to offer solutions. They validate the fear. They share what they know and admit what they don't. But most importantly, they stay grounded, clear, and emotionally steady.

And just like that, a shift begins. Tension gives way to trust. Now anchored in something real, the team starts thinking creatively instead of catastrophically. Solutions rise where before there was just silence.

What these two stories show isn't just good crisis management. It's emotional intelligence in action. Because anyone can lead when the path is smooth, but it takes something deeper to lead when the road is crumbling beneath your feet.

These leaders didn't let fear take the wheel. They paused. They breathed. They understood that how they made people feel in that moment would matter more than any perfect plan. And instead of reacting, they responded with clarity, empathy, and courage.

Emotional intelligence during a crisis isn't about being flawless or fearless. It's about being fully present. It's about knowing that your emotional state will ripple through your entire team, and choosing to signal calm instead of chaos. It's about looking someone in the eye, hearing their concern, and letting them know they're not alone in this mess.

It's not magic. It's self-awareness. It's restraint. And yes, it's appreciation—for the people you lead, the values you stand for, and the impact you want to leave behind.

In the end, these emotionally intelligent decisions didn't just save reputations or financial numbers. They built something more substantial: trust in the brand, the leader, and the team. And that kind of trust doesn't just survive a crisis; it grows stronger because of it.

So, remember what matters most next time you're in the middle of chaos—a company-wide emergency or a team meeting that's gone off the rails. It's not about fixing everything immediately. It's about showing up with your humanity intact. The decisions you make from that space won't just solve problems. They'll inspire people to rise with you.

How Empathy Beat Ego: A Leadership Story That Inspires

Before Alex truly understood emotional intelligence—not just the buzzword version—he would have attributed his boss's behavior to "the cost of working in high-performance environments." Stress, yelling, micromanagement... it was simply part of the job, right?

At least, that's what Tom always said.

Tom was a powerhouse—a marketing executive with a sixth sense for market trends, bold campaigns, and a network that could fund a startup overnight. But he also had a temper that could curdle fresh coffee. Meetings often ended with slammed doors and stunned silence. Team members spoke in cautious tones, tiptoeing around his moods. It wasn't just pressure—it was fear. And it was everywhere.

Alex used to think that staying quiet and efficient was the smart move. Keep your head down, deliver your numbers, and don't poke the bear.

But then came the leadership course—the one on emotional intelligence.

It didn't just change how Alex saw leadership—it changed how he saw *Tom*.

For the first time, Alex understood that Tom wasn't "passionate"—he was emotionally dysregulated. The yelling wasn't driven by passion—it stemmed from a lack of impulse control. The micromanaging wasn't a strategy—it was fear masked as authority. And most importantly, the silence within the team wasn't professionalism; it was survival.

With this new lens, Alex didn't just see the cracks. He felt the impact. Talented colleagues were disengaging. The creative energy that once fueled the team had dried up. People were burnt out, scared to speak and stay, but just as scared to leave. The numbers were still okay, but the soul of the team? That was fading fast.

Alex didn't have a title that gave him power over Tom, but he did have something else: influence.

So, he started small.

When Tom's tone turned sharp in meetings, Alex would stay calm. Grounded. He wouldn't mirror the aggression—he'd slow things down. Ask clarifying questions. Invite others into the conversation. Sometimes, he'd gently steer the group back to the issue instead of the outburst.

Behind the scenes, he checked in with colleagues, not to gossip but to validate. "Hey, I saw how tense that meeting got—just wanted to say your idea was solid." These were little human touches that started stitching back a frayed culture.

He also began managing up carefully. He'd make suggestions to Tom regarding outcomes: "I've noticed we get stronger input when people feel safe to share. Maybe we kick off the next session with open brainstorming?" Sometimes, Tom rolled his eyes. Sometimes, he didn't, but gradually, he listened.

Alex even suggested an outside facilitator for a quarterly planning retreat— "to keep us focused." What he didn't say was that it would give the team a safe space to contribute without Tom's shadow looming over every sentence. The difference was night and day.

And slowly, the tides began to shift.

The team started speaking up again. People smiled more. The walls that fear had built began to crack just enough for trust to start seeping back in. Tom, while far from transformed, had moments of reflection. Maybe it was the mirror Alex held up with his consistent calm. Perhaps it was the quiet influence of someone who led with emotional strength instead of control.

Either way, something was changing.

Alex learned you don't need to be top to lead. You need to know how to manage your emotions, see others clearly, and make choices that protect people's dignity—even when the room feels on fire.

Tom's leadership had become a cautionary tale. But Alex's response? That became a blueprint.

Because emotional intelligence doesn't just protect you from becoming the problem—it empowers you to become part of the solution, even when the boss isn't ready for their transformation.

Alex's quiet influence didn't go unnoticed. Senior leaders—ones outside of Tom's department—started hearing about the turnaround. They started watching Alex—not just for what he was doing but also for *how* he was doing it. He wasn't loud. He wasn't flashy. But he had created a measurable impact, powered by empathy, self-awareness, and emotional strength.

Six months later, Alex was promoted to Director.

Not because he'd made the most noise. But because he had created the most *trust* and transformed a team's culture without ever being its "official" leader.

That's what emotional intelligence does. It elevates everything it touches—teams, results, and *people*.

Alex's story isn't just a lesson in how to survive a bad boss. It's proven that emotional intelligence isn't a soft skill; it's a power skill. One that quietly rewrites your reputation, reshapes your influence, and redefines what leadership looks like.

So, if you're stuck under someone like Tom, don't wait for change. *Be* the change. Because when you lead with emotional intelligence, the room shifts. The culture shifts. And sooner than you think… *your title does too.*

The Cost of Emotionally Unintelligent Leadership

Alex's story had a ripple effect, not just within his team. It revealed something many leaders overlook: when emotional intelligence is absent, the cost isn't just tension or a few bad meetings. It's much deeper. And much more expensive.

Let's pause for a moment and ask: What does a lack of emotional intelligence *really* cost in the workplace?

For Tom's team, the answer showed up in silent meetings, unspoken ideas, and that subtle disengagement you can feel but can't always track on a spreadsheet. It showed up in promising talent walking out the door without a fight. In projects that stalled because people were too afraid to challenge bad decisions. In client relationships that quietly eroded, not because of poor service, but because they sensed internal friction.

These are the hidden losses of emotionally unaware leadership:

- Brilliant ideas that die unspoken
- A culture of compliance instead of creativity
- Teams who do just enough to survive—but never more
- The best employees leaving, and the rest checking out silently

And the financial side? That's real, too.

High turnover increases recruitment and onboarding costs. Burnout raises health-related expenses and absenteeism. Dysfunctional teams are slower to respond, slower to innovate, and slower to deliver.

But perhaps the most significant cost is trust—once it's gone, everything takes twice as long and feels ten times harder.

Ironically, many leaders like Tom don't even see this happening. They're focused on results, numbers, and outcomes. But emotional intelligence lives in the *how*, not just the *what*. How people feel *as they work* directly affects what they can create, solve, and sustain.

When leaders fail to manage their emotions, they silently permit everyone else to do the same. Emotional reactivity becomes the norm, blame becomes the default, and growth is replaced by fear.

That's why Alex's quiet leadership stood out so boldly. He reversed the flow in a world where chaos can trickle from the top down. His emotional intelligence became a stabilizer, and that stability became a magnet for trust, performance, and promotion.

People don't leave companies; they leave leaders lacking emotional intelligence.

And those who stay? They're not always staying for the right reasons.

So, as you reflect on your own leadership, ask yourself:

- *Am I creating a culture people want to grow in, or escape from?*
- *Do my reactions build trust or erode it?*
- *What invisible costs might my emotional blind spots be creating?*

Recognizing the cost is the first step toward transformation. And choosing emotional intelligence isn't just about becoming a better leader.

It's about *stopping the damage* and starting the real work of leading people well.

Leadership Lessons from Emotional Intelligence Failures

Not all leadership lessons come wrapped in praise and success. Some of the most powerful ones come from watching a leader fail—and realizing *that's precisely what I don't want to become.*

Emotional intelligence is often celebrated as a tool for connection, empathy, and influence. But its absence? That's where absolute chaos begins. And that chaos leaves behind valuable clues—lessons etched into the silence of disengaged teams, the sting of high turnover, and the weight of decisions made in emotional fog.

We've all met someone like Tom—a leader with a sharp mind and a short fuse. Tom could sell a vision like no one else, but when the pressure mounted, so did his volume. Feedback became criticism. Accountability turned into blame. And trust? It vanished like smoke.

At first, his team tried to keep up. They thought maybe it was just the cost of working with a "high performer." But fear, once it takes root, can choke out creativity. People stopped speaking up. They second-guessed their ideas. Collaboration suffered. Resentment grew.

And Tom? He didn't notice. Not because he didn't care, but because he lacked *self-awareness*. Emotional intelligence failure starts there—not knowing how your emotions show up, how they affect others, or how they slowly shape your team's culture.

So, what do we learn from watching this unfold?

First: **Emotional outbursts break trust faster than broken promises.**

When leaders can't manage their tempers, they train their team to hide, not to perform. People stop contributing not because they're incapable but because they feel unsafe. One explosion can erase months of effort in building psychological safety.

Second: **Empathy is not a bonus trait—it's the bridge to loyalty.**

Tom's failure to see how his actions landed on others caused a ripple effect. When employees feel unseen, they disengage. When clients sense friction, they look elsewhere. Empathy would've allowed Tom to pause, ask questions, and respond instead of react.

Third: **Emotional blind spots make poor decisions inevitable.**

Tom's emotional hijacking hurt not just his feelings but also his strategy. He made impulsive choices that ignored data, dismissed team input, and created friction between departments. When emotions drive decisions without filters, the business suffers, too.

But the biggest lesson? Emotional intelligence is a leadership multiplier. Its absence doesn't just subtract from performance—it can reverse progress entirely.

Leaders like Alex, who've learned to regulate their emotions, read the room, and lead with intention, become anchors in turbulent times. They don't need to yell to be heard or control to be respected. They lead with presence, not pressure.

And that makes all the difference.

Leadership failures rooted in low emotional intelligence aren't just cautionary tales. They're invitations to lead differently, better, with heart *and* strength. The worst leaders teach us the best lessons—when we're brave enough to listen.

Tailoring Emotional Intelligence to Your Industry

Each industry has unique challenges that require a distinct application of emotional intelligence. Empathy is crucial in customer service. Picture a busy retail store with a frustrated customer—here, empathizing can turn a negative encounter into loyalty. Staff who apply emotional intelligence diffuse tension, offer solutions, and leave customers feeling heard, often becoming the difference between retaining or losing clientele.

Customization is key. Leaders should develop emotional intelligence practices aligned with their industry's core values. In hospitality, training might focus on service recovery through empathy; in tech, on collaboration and problem-solving. Tailoring emotional intelligence ensures teams are ready to meet specific challenges effectively.

The benefits are tangible. A healthcare facility might see better patient satisfaction and staff retention; a manufacturing company might see improved teamwork and efficiency. Tailored emotional intelligence solves industry pain points and builds a competitive advantage.

Consider retail: One leader prioritized empathy and active listening training, transforming the shopping experience. Customers felt appreciated, increasing repeat business, enhancing employee pride, and raising sales and morale.

Incorporating industry-specific emotional intelligence starts with understanding your field's unique dynamics. Leaders should identify areas for improvement, conduct assessments, and collaborate with experts to design effective programs. The payoff? Higher employee engagement, customer satisfaction, and team performance.

One size does not fit all. Tailoring your approach enhances leadership, empowers teams, and drives long-term success.

As we transition into the next chapter, we will explore how emotional intelligence fosters innovation and creativity, two critical elements for success in any industry. Through this exploration, you'll discover new ways to inspire your team and elevate your leadership impact further.

TOP 3 TAKEAWAYS
(CHAPTER 7)

1   Your emotional tone sets the temperature for the room.

In a crisis, people don't just follow your words—they absorb your presence. If you stay calm, grounded, and clear, your team will too. Emotional intelligence isn't about being flawless—it's about showing up steady when it matters most.

2   Crisis reveals what kind of leader you are.

Under pressure, emotionally intelligent leaders don't scramble—they listen, adapt, and lead with presence. They know when to pause, when to speak, and when to create space for others to contribute. Crisis doesn't build character—it exposes it.

3   The cost of ignoring emotional intelligence is real.

Without EQ, trust cracks, tension rises, and decisions are driven by fear instead of focus. Talented people check out, collaboration stalls, and culture quietly erode. In crisis, emotional intelligence isn't optional—it's the edge that keeps your team from falling apart.

Chapter 8: Sustaining Growth and Continuous Learning

"Leadership and learning are indispensable to each other."
— John F. Kennedy

You've done the hard work—built emotional intelligence, led with heart, and seen real results. But outstanding leadership doesn't rest. If emotional intelligence got you here, growth is what keeps you moving forward. And not just any growth—intentional, evolving, and rooted in curiosity.

Emotional intelligence isn't a static skillset; it's more like a muscle that strengthens with use. What worked when your team was five people might not hold up when you're leading fifty. That's why sustaining your growth means committing to continuous learning—not just for your team, but for yourself.

This chapter is about staying sharp, staying relevant, and staying human. It's about building a personal growth plan that matches your ambition. It's about learning not just from wins and losses, but from new trends, new research, and new ways of seeing the same challenge.

It's also about positioning emotional intelligence as more than a "nice-to-have." In high-performing organizations, it's a core leadership competency—and a competitive edge. Whether advancing your career or shaping a more emotionally intelligent culture, your growth mindset becomes your guide.

So, let's dive in. In the pages ahead, you'll learn how to turn reflection into action, growth into strategy, and emotional intelligence into your long-term leadership advantage.

Creating a Personal Growth Plan for Emotional Intelligence

Starting your emotional intelligence growth journey? Think of it as designing a roadmap—not just to "be better," but to grow smarter, lead wiser, and connect deeper. This isn't a one-size-fits-all plan; it's personal, purposeful, and designed around your real-life leadership moments.

Begin by identifying the areas that need attention. Do you react too quickly under pressure? Do you struggle to empathize with others' perspectives truly? These honest reflections are your launchpad.

Awareness isn't just the first step—it's the fuel that drives meaningful change.

Next, set goals that are clear, practical, and measurable. Swap vague intentions like "be more empathetic" for something focused: "practice active listening in team meetings by summarizing what others say before responding." These micro-targets help you track progress and celebrate the wins, because progress deserves applause, even in small doses.

Your growth plan should also include intentional learning. Workshops and structured courses can deepen your skills, while books and articles offer expert insights to expand your thinking. These aren't just resources but strategic tools in your leadership arsenal.

Don't do it alone. Find an accountability partner or mentor who will challenge you, cheer for you, and keep you honest. Regular check-ins can shift your perspective and reignite motivation when things get tough. Growth is always better with a guide.

Keep it dynamic. Review your plan every few months. If you've mastered a goal, set a new one. If you've hit a wall, adjust. Your plan should evolve like you do—as a leader, a learner, and a human being.

Growth isn't about perfection; it's about being just a little more emotionally intelligent tomorrow than you were today.

Continuous Feedback Loops: Learning From Your Team

Growth isn't a one-time event—it's a cycle. And some of the most powerful insights that fuel your leadership development come from one of the richest sources around: your team.

But here's the shift—in this stage of your journey, feedback isn't just about fixing issues or offering encouragement. It's about learning in real time, adapting continuously, and creating an environment where growth is mutual and ongoing.

Emotionally intelligent leaders treat feedback as a learning loop—a rhythm that keeps the team evolving together. They don't just collect input—they use it as a compass for what's next: new skills to develop, gaps to close, and mindsets to shift.

- ✓ **Make Learning a Two-Way Street**

By this point in your leadership, your role isn't just to lead—it's to learn alongside your team. Feedback becomes part of your team's collective intelligence, revealing emerging needs, hidden talents, and even early signs of burnout or disengagement. When you position feedback as a shared learning process rather than a performance checkpoint, you build a culture that thrives on curiosity and growth.

Try asking:

- What's one thing we've recently learned we should build on?

- What should we unlearn or rethink based on what's not working anymore?

These questions turn day-to-day work into ongoing education for everyone involved.

✓ Keep It Embedded, Not Episodic

Annual reviews won't cut it. Feedback needs to be baked into your leadership's rhythm to truly support continuous learning. Use retrospectives, end-of-project reflections, and even team Slack channels as places where micro-lessons surface. These bite-sized insights are gold when gathered consistently.

Want to build a more resilient, agile team? Make it normal to reflect as you go, not just when something breaks.

✓ Action Is the Ultimate Learning Tool

What turns feedback into growth isn't just hearing it—it's what you do with it. When you act on insights from your team, you model humility, adaptability, and forward-thinking.

Even small changes based on team input show that you're responsive and evolving. That builds psychological safety and encourages others to stay engaged in the process.

Staying Current: Emotional Intelligence Trends and Research

Emotional intelligence isn't a fixed trait—it's a living, breathing field of insight that continues evolving alongside how we work, lead, and connect. In today's fast-moving landscape, staying informed isn't just helpful—it's a leadership necessity.

We no longer operate in the same environment that birthed classic EQ models. With the rise of hybrid teams, AI tools, and digital communication, how we express—and interpret—emotion has changed. For example, neuroscience now explores how our brains respond to emotional cues over screens, and how leaders can foster empathy when facial expressions are filtered through pixels or Slack emojis. Staying current means learning how to lead in these evolving spaces without losing the human touch.

> ***What's Shifting Right Now?***

Here are a few emerging trends worth tracking:

- **Digital EQ**: Research reveals how emotionally intelligent behaviors appear in virtual environments. Leaders are learning to "read the room" through tone of voice, response timing, and emoji use.
- **AI and Empathy**: As artificial intelligence becomes a workplace companion, leaders must distinguish between automation and connection. The rising question: *What should be handled by humans, and how do we ensure it feels human?*

- **Well-being as Strategy**: Emotional intelligence is now closely linked to organizational wellness. Studies show that EQ-driven leadership correlates with lower burnout, higher retention, and more psychologically safe environments.

How to Stay Sharp (Without Burning Out)

You don't need to wade through academic journals to stay current. Try this more sustainable learning strategy:

- **Curate your sources**: Subscribe to 1–2 newsletters from trusted thought leaders (e.g. Daniel Goleman's Emotional Intelligence Coaching Network or Harvard Business Review's leadership digest).
- **Choose one trend to follow per quarter**: Instead of chasing every headline, go deep on a single theme, like digital empathy or resilience practices, and test it within your team.
- **Pair new research with a reflection habit**: After you learn something new, ask yourself:

How does this challenge or confirm how I lead? Where can I apply it this week? Reflection turns insight into action.

Keep asking the hard questions and stay open to being surprised. Every new insight sharpens your impact, and that kind of leadership leaves a legacy.

3 Must-Follow Sources for EQ Trends

1. **Daniel Goleman's Emotional Intelligence Coaching Network**
   Why follow: Goleman practically coined the term *EQ*. His articles and podcasts translate cutting-edge research into practical leadership insights.

   https://www.linkedin.com/newsletters/6727923233074487296/

2. **Harvard Business Review (HBR) – Emotional Intelligence Section**
   Why follow: HBR blends science and leadership wisdom, offering data-backed strategies on emotional intelligence, resilience, and communication.

   https://hbr.org/search?term=emotional+intelligence

3. **Six Seconds – The Emotional Intelligence Network**
   Why follow: This nonprofit provides global research, free toolkits, and practical frameworks for EQ in leadership, education, and team performance.

   https://www.6seconds.org/articles/

Tip: Choose one to explore deeply each month. Bookmark articles, take notes, and reflect on how the insight applies to your team's current reality.

Leveraging Emotional Intelligence for Career Advancement

When it comes to career growth, technical skills may get you a foot in the door, but emotional intelligence is what opens the next one. As industries evolve and leadership roles demand more relational dexterity, emotional intelligence has become one of the most sought-after differentiators. It signals not just competence but readiness for impact.

In workplaces where expertise is often evenly matched, what sets future leaders apart is their ability to navigate complex relationships, resolve tension with empathy, and foster psychological safety. These aren't just "soft skills"—they're career catalysts.

Want to stand out in performance reviews, team meetings, or stakeholder conversations? Bring emotional intelligence into the spotlight—not as a concept, but as evidence. Share examples of how you de-escalated a high-stakes conflict, turned disengagement into motivation, or coached a struggling colleague with empathy and results.

These aren't humblebrags—they're proof points. They show that you're not just leading projects; you're leading people with emotional agility.

Networking isn't just about swapping cards or adding contacts. It's about making authentic impressions, and emotional intelligence gives you the edge. You create lasting connections when you read a room accurately, tailor your tone to match your audience, or show genuine interest in someone else's perspective. And let's be honest: *people advocate for people they connect with.*

Leaders who use emotional intelligence to grow their careers know that self-awareness and reflection aren't optional—they're ongoing strategies. Take time to audit your behaviors:

- When do you default to reactivity over reflection?
- How often do you adapt your communication based on the other person's cues?
- What emotional habits have served you—or held you back?

The answers reveal how you show up—and how you can grow smarter from here.

Career advancement fueled by emotional intelligence isn't just about climbing higher—it's about moving better: with clarity, compassion, and conviction. It deepens your relationships, sharpens your judgment, and builds a reputation that invites trust.

In a world hungry for connection and credibility, emotional intelligence isn't just a way to stand out—it's how you rise with impact.

TOP 3 TAKEAWAYS
(CHAPTER 8)

1   Emotional Intelligence Is a Muscle—Flex It Daily.

You don't "arrive" at emotional intelligence. You build, stretch, and adapt it as your leadership grows. What worked yesterday won't always work tomorrow. Keep evolving or risk becoming irrelevant.

2   Feedback isn't a threat—it's your growth strategy.

The most innovative leaders aren't the ones who know it all; they're the ones who keep learning, especially from their team. Turn every project, mistake, or meeting into a mini-masterclass. Learning loops = leadership gold.

3   Without EQ, Growth Stalls—And So Does Your Team.

Emotional intelligence evolves—and so should you. When leaders stop learning, their EQ and team energy go stale. Staying current with new research, trends, and tools isn't optional—it's how you keep leading with relevance and impact.

Conclusion

Lead With Heart. Grow With Intention.

As you turn the final pages of this book, take a moment to breathe in how far you've come.

Together, we've explored the heart of emotional intelligence—self-awareness, emotion regulation, empathy, communication, conflict resolution, cultural sensitivity, and the courage to keep evolving. These aren't just leadership ideals but fundamental tools for real moments—tools that shift how you show up for yourself and your team.

You saw what happens when leaders dare to lead differently through Sarah and Alex. Sarah learned to slow down and connect. Alex discovered that empathy wasn't weakness—it was his breakthrough. Their growth wasn't perfect, but it was powerful, just like yours can be.

In a world where technical skill may get you in the door, emotional intelligence keeps you in the room—and helps everyone rise with you.

You now hold strategies to:

- Navigate tension with calm,
- Foster trust with intention,
- And build teams that feel heard, seen, and inspired to give their best.

But this isn't the end. Emotional intelligence isn't a box you check. It's a practice, a mindset, a lifelong journey.

Keep learning. Keep listening. Keep leading with both courage and care.

Your next meeting, conversation, or decision is another chance to practice what you've learned. And with every step, you're not just becoming a better leader—you're becoming a more grounded, impactful, and human.

Thank you for taking this journey. And remember:

The most powerful leaders aren't the ones who speak the loudest—
but the ones who listen the deepest.

Lead on.

You can reach me at: gjaureguikarina@gmail.com

Follow me on Medium for more insights, stories, and practical advice to empower your professional growth.

Together, we can inspire change and shape a more inclusive future!

You've Done the Inner Work—Now Share the Journey
Leave a Review. Inspire a Leader.

Thank you for investing in yourself and choosing to lead with emotional intelligence, strength, and heart.
Now, imagine how your words could encourage someone else to do the same.

Was there a moment that moved you? A tool you'll carry into every meeting? A shift in how you see yourself or your team?

If so, share it. A short review on Amazon, Goodreads, or your favorite platform can make a big difference. Your insight might be the nudge another leader needs to begin this journey.

Together, we're creating a world of courageous, emotionally intelligent leadership—one brave voice at a time.

Thank you for being part of it.

MORE BOOKS BY KARINA G. JAUREGUI:

The Power of Women In Leadership

Step Into Your Power and Lead with Confidence, Purpose, and Authenticity

Whether you're aiming for your next big promotion, stepping into a leadership role for the first time, or seeking to strengthen your skills as a seasoned manager, **this is your moment to rise.**

The Power of Women in Leadership is a motivating, practical guide for professional women ready to lead with clarity, courage, and balance. It offers proven tools and actionable strategies to help you own your voice, elevate your impact, and grow your career, **without compromising your values or well-being.**

Inside, you'll learn how to:

- Speak up and be heard—even in male-dominated environments
- Conquer imposter syndrome and lead with unshakable self-belief
- Navigate workplace politics with confidence and integrity
- Create real work-life balance—without guilt or burnout
- Build strong networks, find mentors, and attract sponsors
- Lead authentically while staying true to your purpose
- Excel as a new manager with practical, people-first leadership strategies

This book is more than a leadership guide—it's a call to action for women ready to lead boldly and authentically.

Available on Amazon, IngramSpark and Audible!

REFERENCES

1. tsw.co.uk. (Daniel goleman emotional intelligence). Retrieved from https://www.tsw.co.uk/blog/leadership-and-management/daniel-goleman-emotional-intelligence/

2. rewireforsuccess.com.au. (Neurological basis of emotional intelligence). Retrieved from https://rewireforsuccess.com.au/neuroscience/neurological-basis-of-emotional-intelligence/

3. mastersinminds.com. (Case study. leaders with high emotional intelligence blog 1). Retrieved from https://www.mastersinminds.com/case-study.-leaders-with-high-emotional-intelligence---blog-1#:~:text=1)Sundar%20Pichai%2C%20CEO%20of,high%20emotional%20intelligence%20(EQ).

4. psico-smart.com. (Blog the role of emotional intelligence in modern leadership development 172217). Retrieved from https://psico-smart.com/en/blogs/blog-the-role-of-emotional-intelligence-in-modern-leadership-development-172217

5. pmc.ncbi.nlm.nih.gov. (Pmc10543214). Retrieved from https://pmc.ncbi.nlm.nih.gov/articles/PMC10543214/

6. forbes.com. (How self awareness elevates leadership effectiveness). Retrieved from https://www.forbes.com/sites/paolacecchi-

dimeglio/2024/02/14/how-self-awareness-elevates-leadership-effectiveness/

7. ccl.org. (Mindfulness a simple way to lead better). Retrieved from https://www.ccl.org/articles/leading-effectively-articles/mindfulness-a-simple-way-to-lead-better/

8. verywellmind.com. (How you can practice self regulation 4163536). Retrieved from https://www.verywellmind.com/how-you-can-practice-self-regulation-4163536

9. online.hbs.edu. (Emotional intelligence in leadership). Retrieved from https://online.hbs.edu/blog/post/emotional-intelligence-in-leadership

10. expirationreminder.com. (10 effective stress management techniques for leaders). Retrieved from https://www.expirationreminder.com/blog/10-effective-stress-management-techniques-for-leaders

11. forbes.com. (17 ways leaders can practice mindfulness to keep calm on busy days). Retrieved from https://www.forbes.com/councils/forbescoachescouncil/2023/08/22/17-ways-leaders-can-practice-mindfulness-to-keep-calm-on-busy-days/

12. lifecoachtraining.co. (Resilience and mental toughness case studies and success stories). Retrieved from https://lifecoachtraining.co/resilience-and-mental-toughness-case-studies-and-success-stories/

13. ccl.org. (Coaching others use active listening skills). Retrieved from https://www.ccl.org/articles/leading-effectively-articles/coaching-others-use-active-listening-skills/

14. insperity.com. (Authentic relationships at work). Retrieved from https://www.insperity.com/blog/authentic-relationships-at-work/

15. culturepartners.com. (Empathetic leadership strategies and tips for driving accountability and improving company culture). Retrieved from https://culturepartners.com/insights/empathetic-leadership-strategies-and-tips-for-driving-accountability-and-improving-company-culture/

16. hbr.org. (Manage a difficult conversation with emotional intelligence). Retrieved from https://hbr.org/2014/06/manage-a-difficult-conversation-with-emotional-intelligence

17. park.edu. (Conflict resolution strategies every leader should master). Retrieved from https://www.park.edu/blog/conflict-resolution-strategies-every-leader-should-master/

18. globalmindfulsolutions.com. (Emotional intelligence and workplace conflict resolution). Retrieved from https://globalmindfulsolutions.com/emotional-intelligence-and-workplace-conflict-resolution/

19. mark-bridges.medium.com. (12 case studies showcasing effective conflict management in the workplace dbdc3ee1140a). Retrieved from https://mark-bridges.medium.com/12-case-studies-showcasing-effective-conflict-management-in-the-workplace-dbdc3ee1140a

20. extensishr.com. (5 ways to foster an open communication office culture). Retrieved from https://extensishr.com/resource/blogs/5-ways-to-foster-an-open-communication-office-culture/

21. ei4change.com. (How emotional intelligence can enhance cross cultural communication). Retrieved from https://ei4change.com/how-emotional-intelligence-can-enhance-cross-cultural-communication/

22. pressbooks.palni.org. (Chapter 2). Retrieved from https://pressbooks.palni.org/diorgculture/chapter/chapter-2/

23. forbes.com. (20 tips for addressing unconscious bias in the workplace starting from the top down). Retrieved from https://www.forbes.com/councils/forbeshumanresourcescouncil/2024/09/13/20-tips-for-addressing-unconscious-bias-in-the-workplace-starting-from-the-top-down/

24. jointhecollective.com. (The role of empathy in cross cultural leadership). Retrieved from https://www.jointhecollective.com/article/the-role-of-empathy-in-cross-cultural-leadership/

25. 6seconds.org. (Case study emotional intelligence people first leadership fedex express). Retrieved from https://www.6seconds.org/2014/01/14/case-study-emotional-intelligence-people-first-leadership-fedex-express/

26. medium.com. (The power of emotional intelligence lessons from microsofts satya nadella eq trumps iq 743bf6777e7b). Retrieved from https://medium.com/@Abir_Chermiti/the-power-of-emotional-intelligence-lessons-from-microsofts-satya-nadella-eq-trumps-iq-743bf6777e7b

27. linkedin.com. (How emotional intelligence enhances crisis management leadership y5wzc). Retrieved from https://www.linkedin.com/pulse/how-emotional-intelligence-enhances-crisis-management-leadership-y5wzc

28. michaelpage.co.uk. (Importance emotional intelligence finance). Retrieved from https://www.michaelpage.co.uk/our-expertise/banking-and-financial-services/importance-emotional-intelligence-finance

29. ccl.org. (Emotional intelligence and leadership effectiveness). Retrieved from https://www.ccl.org/articles/leading-effectively-articles/emotional-intelligence-and-leadership-effectiveness/

30. linkedin.com. (How do you create implement personal development). Retrieved from https://www.linkedin.com/advice/3/how-do-you-create-implement-personal-development

31. linkedin.com. (Harnessing feedback loops enhancing leadership growth netish sharma wjzac). Retrieved from https://www.linkedin.com/pulse/harnessing-feedback-loops-enhancing-leadership-growth-netish-sharma-wjzac

32. frontiersin.org. (Magazine). Retrieved from https://www.frontiersin.org/research-topics/26568/new-trends-in-emotional-intelligence-conceptualization-understanding-and-assessment/magazine

www.ingramcontent.com/pod-product-compliance
Lightning Source LLC
LaVergne TN
LVHW012023060526
838201LV00061B/4424